EXPERIENCING A
MIGHTY
CHANGE OF HEART

ALMA'S GUIDE TO A DEEP, LASTING CONVERSION

D1603057

OTHER BOOKS AND AUDIOBOOKS BY ED J. PINEGAR

Press Forward Saints
Living by the Word
Your Patriarchal Blessing
Happily Ever After
Power Tools for Missionaries, Four Volumes
After Your Mission
Lengthen Your Shuffle
Series of Latter-day Commentaries, Teachings and Commentaries,
Unlocking, and Who's Who—Old Testament, New Testament, Book of
Mormon, and Doctrine and Covenants
The Temple: Gaining Knowledge and Power in the House of the Lord
The Christmas Code
The Christmas List
Preparing for the Melchizedek Priesthood and My Mission
The Little Book of Gratitude
31 Days to a Better You
Fatherhood: A Calling of Love
It's Great to Be a Missionary
Living after the Manner of Happiness
Because of Him
God the Father

OTHER BOOKS AND AUDIOBOOKS BY JOHN W. WELCH

Knowing Why: 137 Evidences That the Book of Mormon Is True
The Parables of Jesus: Revealing the Plan of Salvation
Knowing Why: 127 MORE Evidences That the Book of Mormon Is True
Reexploring the Book of Mormon
The Legal Cases in the Book of Mormon
Glimpses of Lehi's Jerusalem
The Tree of Life: From Eden to Eternity
King Benjamin's Speech
Chiasmus in Antiquity
Illuminating the Sermon at the Temple and Sermon on the Mount
Opening the Heavens
Joseph Smith's Legal Encounters

EXPERIENCING A
MIGHTY
CHANGE OF HEART

ALMA'S GUIDE TO A DEEP, LASTING CONVERSION

ED J. PINEGAR &
JOHN W. WELCH

Covenant Communications, Inc.

Cover images: *Marble with Golden Texture Background Vector Illustration* © vectortwins, Shutterstock; *Luxury Vector Collection of Polygonal Hearts. Invitation Template. Set Geometric Shape.* © Dmitry Kostrov, iStock

Cover design by Kimberly Kay copyright © 2020 by Covenant Communications, Inc.

Published by Covenant Communications, Inc.
American Fork, Utah

Printed in the United States of America
First Printing: March 2020

27 26 25 24 23 22 21 20   10 9 8 7 6 5 4 3 2 1

ISBN: 978-1-52441-287-6

ACKNOWLEDGMENTS

WE ARE DEEPLY GRATEFUL IN many ways, to numerous people, for their valuable assistance in making this book possible.

We are thankful for Alma and for his desire to know these eternal truths for himself through fasting and prayer and by the power of the Holy Spirit of God.

We acknowledge the Lord God, who made these things known to Alma by His Holy Spirit and through the spirit of revelation.

We stand in awe at the unparalleled miracle, brought forth in April 1829, by the 23-year-old Prophet Joseph Smith, as he translated Alma's inspiring words by the gift and power of God.

We eagerly recognize the many authors quoted within these pages who have insightfully added understandings to these precious doctrines.

We are particularly indebted to special friends and colleagues whose significant input has generously helped during the process of creating this book.

We are also much obliged to the faithful editors at Covenant Communications, especially Ashley Gebert and Samantha Milburn. Their untiring efforts have made the manuscript better in every way.

We bless our beloved and sensitive wives, Jeannie S. Welch and Patricia P. Pinegar, for their wisdom and dedicated support.

We warmly welcome our readers, be they devoted teachers, seekers after knowledge, dependable mentors, or loving family members, for opening these pages and bringing them to life.

And for all of this, we praise our kind Father in Heaven and our Savior Jesus Christ, in all possible times and ways, for Their unfailing grace and goodness.

TABLE OF CONTENTS

CHAPTER ONE

INTRODUCING ALMA'S GREATEST SPEECH

I speak by way of command unto you that belong to the church; and unto those who do not belong to the church I speak by way of invitation, saying: Come and be baptized unto repentance, that ye also may be partakers of the fruit of the tree of life. (Alma 5:62)

THE PROPHETS HAVE PREACHED REPENTANCE since the beginning of time. President Russell M. Nelson in the 2019 April general conference stated,

> Recently I have found myself drawn to the Lord's instruction given through the Prophet Joseph Smith: "Say nothing but repentance unto this generation." This declaration is often repeated throughout scripture [such as in Mosiah 18:20; 25:22; Helaman 13:6; Doctrine and Covenants 6:9; and 11:9]. It prompts an obvious question: "Does *everyone* need to repent?" The answer is yes.
>
> Too many people consider repentance as punishment—something to be avoided except in the most serious circumstances. But this feeling of being penalized is engendered by Satan. He tries to block us from looking to Jesus Christ, who stands with open arms, hoping and willing to heal, forgive, cleanse, strengthen, purify, and sanctify us.
>
> The word for *repentance* in the Greek New Testament is *metanoeō*. The prefix *meta-* means "change." The suffix *-noeō* is related to Greek words that mean "mind," "knowledge," "spirit," and "breath."
>
> Thus, when Jesus asks you and me to "repent," He is inviting us to change our mind, our knowledge, our spirit—

even the way we breathe. He is asking us to change the way we love, think, serve, spend our time, treat our wives, teach our children, and even care for our bodies.

Nothing is more liberating, more ennobling, or more crucial to our individual progression than is a regular, daily focus on repentance. Repentance is not an event; it is a process. It is the key to happiness and peace of mind. When coupled with faith, repentance opens our access to the power of the Atonement of Jesus Christ.[1]

Alma tried to do all he could to reclaim his people from straying from the covenant path. Alma 5 records what is, for many reasons, Alma's greatest public speech. That's quite a statement; this is a prophet who taught and prophesied and preached repentance for somewhere between two and three decades. His ministry began when, as a wicked and idolatrous man who had tried to destroy the Church,[2] he was visited by an angel who told him to "go thy way, and seek to destroy the church no more" (Mosiah 27:16). The experience was, as we can imagine, both shattering and astonishing. From that time forward, he became one of the best-known teachers of faith among all God's prophets. He never stopped preaching until "the saying went abroad in the church that he was taken up by the Spirit, or buried by the hand of the Lord, even as Moses" (Alma 45:19).

For at least twenty-five years, Alma spoke to countless people, teaching the doctrines of Christ and preaching repentance. He spoke encouragingly about the Atonement of Christ to the righteous people in Gideon.[3] He called the wicked people in Ammonihah to repentance and deliverance,[4] and in a last-ditch effort to turn them away from their Nehorite ways, Alma spoke to them urgently about spiritual death, probation, and the plan of redemption,[5] followed by his testimony about the high priesthood after the holy order of the Son of God.[6] On the occasion of the fiftieth year after King Benjamin's speech, and after being reunited with the four sons of Mosiah after fourteen years apart, Alma wrote the beautiful words, "O that I were an angel . . . and could speak with the trump of God . . ." (Alma 29:1). Addressing the Zoramite

---

1   Russell M. Nelson, "We Can Do Better and Be Better," *Ensign* or *Liahona,* May 2019.
2   See Mosiah 27:8.
3   See Alma 7.
4   See Alma 9.
5   See Alma 12.
6   See Alma 13.

poor who had been cast out of Antionum, Alma poured out his heart about humility, faith, prayer, and the Atonement of Jesus Christ.[7] Privately, he taught and blessed his three sons, Helaman,[8] Shiblon,[9] and Corianton,[10] speaking to them powerfully about his conversion, following the Lord, being wise, and understanding sin, redemption, justice, mercy, resurrection, and restoration.

What, then, makes the discourse recorded in Alma 5 the greatest of his ministry? In this inaugural speech, given right after Alma had turned his sole attention to his duties as the high priest in the land of Zarahemla, Alma addressed everyone. He spoke with the energy of his whole soul[11] to pose fifty life-changing questions—asking his covenant people gathered in Zarahemla, as well as us who read his words in our day—to examine the very way we live. It is here that Alma speaks directly to the soul of every listener. On the occasion of Alma 5, he boldly details the weightier matters of God's laws of salvation and eternal life. Because the Book of Mormon tells us the original setting and purpose of this speech,[12] we can confidently understand and interpret its words in context. It is not a philosophical discourse. It is not an esoteric or abstract treatise. It was delivered as ecclesiastic instruction from the highest priesthood leader of the Church. It was aimed at unifying and regulating the whole body of the Church by inspiring and enabling the righteousness and worthiness of each individual member. It is through that lens that Alma 5 can most authentically and effectively be read and applied today.

While Alma's speech is infused with a powerful plea to repent, it goes beyond that crucial point to ask a spectrum of thought-provoking queries and then to offer eloquent discussions of—among other things—personal conversion, a mighty change of heart, deliverance, personal revelation, the Lord's Atonement, and preparing to meet God—all fruits of repentance. Here he reaches the personal heart of each individual who desires to be a disciple of the Lord Jesus Christ.

Come, Follow Me—For Individuals and Families begins under the title "Conversion Is Our Goal":

> The aim of all gospel learning and teaching is to deepen our conversion and help us become more like Jesus Christ. For

---

7   See Alma 32–33.
8   See Alma 36–37.
9   See Alma 38.
10   See Alma 39–42.
11   See Alma 5:43.
12   See Alma 4:19; 6:1–6.

this reason, when we study the gospel, we're not just looking for new information; we want to become a "new creature" (see 2 Corinthians 5:17). This means relying on Christ to change our hearts, our views, our actions, and our very natures.[13]

Becoming "a new creature" is the sum and substance of much of Alma's masterful discourse—the repentance that precedes it, the conversion process that enables it, and the faith that sustains it. Echoing throughout the entire discourse is the role of the Holy Ghost in facilitating every part of it. The rhetorical questions delivered by Alma required deep introspection and pondering, for the people in his Zarahemla audience were struggling. Regardless of our individual condition, these questions require the same introspection and pondering of us.

It is instructive to realize that Alma knew his listeners very well. He had grown up with these people; he had worked with them for nine years as both their high priest and their chief judge. He had personally led them to victory in a bloody civil war, in which many had died. Perhaps it could be argued that he knew the people *too* well. But as we read his address in Alma 5, we see with profound clarity that his greatest desire was to bring them to repentance and help them stay on the covenant path. Alma had a great love for the people despite their challenges—a quality exhibited by every great leader. He wanted them to succeed. Regardless of how stern his remarks may seem at certain times, it is always easy to sense Alma's love, and the way in which he reflects the love of the Savior, for the people.

To set the context of Alma 5, we need to consider what was happening during the previous as well as subsequent chapters. Several factors had combined to lead to the spiritual decline of the people in Zarahemla. Many of them were too young to have heard King Benjamin's soul-changing address[14] that was delivered forty-two years earlier and that served as a catalyst for the conversion of all those in Zarahemla who heard it. In fact, we are told that King Benjamin

> thought it was expedient, after having finished speaking to the people, that he should take the names of all those who had entered into a covenant with God to keep his commandments.
>
> And it came to pass that there was *not one soul*, except it were little children, but who had entered into the covenant and had taken upon them the name of Christ. (Mosiah 6:1–2; emphasis added)

---

13 *Come Follow Me—For Individuals and Families.* 2019.
14 See Mosiah 2–5.

Not having personally heard King Benjamin's stirring discourse, the people Alma faced in Zarahemla had grown much less inclined to be religious; in fact, many of Alma's listeners had "yielded [themselves] to become subjects to the devil" (Alma 5:20). While King Benjamin had been able to place all his listeners under covenant to obey the commandments, Alma faced a much different situation at the conclusion of his address. Those listeners who refused to repent and humble themselves before God were excommunicated: "their names were blotted out, that their names were not numbered among those of the righteous" (Alma 6:3).

Another factor leading to the decline of the Church in Zarahemla during Alma's reign was a general increase in pride;[15] the law of consecration was no longer being observed because of pride and contention among the members of the Church. In fact, the rapid decline of the Church over a brief two-year period was attributed to the material prosperity of the Church:

> And it came to pass in the eighth year of the reign of the judges, that the people of the church began to wax proud, because of their exceeding riches, and their fine silks, and their fine-twined linen, and because of their many flocks and herds, and their gold and their silver, and all manner of precious things, which they had obtained by their industry; and in all these things were they lifted up in the pride of their eyes, for they began to wear very costly apparel.
>
> Now this was the cause of much affliction to Alma, yea, and to many of the people whom Alma had consecrated to be teachers, and priests, and elders over the church; yea, many of them were sorely grieved for the wickedness which they saw had begun to be among their people.
>
> For they saw and beheld with great sorrow that the people of the church began to be lifted up in the pride of their eyes, and to set their hearts upon riches and upon the vain things of the world, that they began to be scornful, one towards another, and they began to persecute those that did not believe according to their own will and pleasure. (Alma 4:6–8)

As a result of their prideful attitudes, the people not only offended some members of the Church, but also those who were not members of the Church,

---

15   See Alma 4:11–13.

becoming "a great stumbling-block to those who did not belong to the church; and thus the church began to fail in its progress" (Alma 4:10). Alma's distress over the condition of the Church undoubtedly informed the tone of his address to the people of Zarahemla.

That distress was so great, in fact, that Alma talked about the people of Zarahemla to the people of Gideon in a later address, referring to "the awful dilemma that our brethren were in at Zarahemla" (Alma 7:3). Reflecting on his experience in Zarahemla, Alma told the people in Gideon, "I trust that ye are not in a state of so much unbelief as were your brethren; I trust that ye are not lifted up in the pride of your hearts; yea, I trust that ye have not set your hearts upon riches and the vain things of the world; yea, I trust that you do not worship idols, but that ye do worship the true and the living God" (Alma 7:6).

Alma occupied the judgment seat as the first elected chief judge over the Nephites, making him the leading government official. During his reign, the Nephites were forced into war, first by the Amlicites and then by an army consisting of both Amlicites and Lamanites.[16] The Nephites claimed victory in each war, but at great internal cost.

During the sixth year of the reign of judges over the people of Nephi, under Alma's rule, Zarahemla saw no more war. But even with a lack of conflict, the people struggled to recover from the wars that had taken place during the previous year, being "greatly afflicted for the loss of their brethren, and also for the loss of their flocks and herds, and also for the loss of their fields of grain, which were trodden under foot and destroyed by the Lamanites" (Alma 4:2).

As so often happens, struggling led to a positive outcome:

> And so great were their afflictions that every soul had cause to mourn; and they believed that it was the judgments of God sent upon them because of their wickedness and their abominations; therefore they were awakened to a remembrance of their duty.
>
> And they began to establish the church more fully; yea, and many were baptized in the waters of Sidon and were joined to the church of God; yea, they were baptized by the hand of Alma, who had been consecrated the high priest over the people of the church, by the hand of his father Alma. (Alma 4:3–4)

While serving simultaneously as the Nephites' chief judge and as the Church's high priest, Alma the Younger faced demanding challenges. He had

---

16   See Alma 2–4.

the power and authority associated with the judgment seat and was expected to arbitrate civil disputes; sadly, his position was threatened by those who sought to use politics for their own gain. As high priest, Alma was also expected to oversee the spiritual concerns of the Nephites and to administer all Church affairs—but unfortunately, the Church was also being threatened by those who sought to use religion to their advantage. Adding to that strain was Alma's increasing concern over the declining spirituality of his people.

In a move that undoubtedly surprised many, after nine years of serving as chief judge over the people of Nephi, Alma stepped aside as directed by the Holy Spirit and delivered the judgment seat to a man named Nephihah.[17] As the scriptures describe him, Nephihah was "a wise man who was among the elders of the church" (Alma 4:16). As Alma's successor to the judgment-seat, and according to the voice of the people, Nephihah had "power to enact laws according to the laws which had been given, and to put them in force according to the wickedness and the crimes of the people" (Alma 4:16). Alma's choice of successor was a good one. We are told that Nephihah "filled the judgment-seat with perfect uprightness before God" (Alma 50:37) until his death sixteen years later.

With Nephihah installed as chief judge, Alma retained his office as chief high priest:

> And this he did that he himself might go forth among his people, or among the people of Nephi, that he might preach the word of God unto them, to stir them up in remembrance of their duty, and that he might pull down, by the word of God, all the pride and craftiness and all the contentions which were among his people, seeing no way that he might reclaim them save it were in bearing down in pure testimony against them. (Alma 4:19)

It's important that we understand exactly what *the office of high priest* is.

> God's chief representative on earth, the one who holds the highest spiritual position in his kingdom in any age, is called *the high priest.* This special designation of the chief spiritual officer of the Church has reference to the administrative position which he holds rather than to the office to which he is ordained in the priesthood.[18]

---

17 See Alma 4:20.
18 Bruce R. McConkie, *Mormon Doctrine*, 2nd ed. (Salt Lake City: Bookcraft, 1966), 355–356.

As the chief high priest, Alma now could focus more exclusively on presiding over the teachings, ordinances, and sacrifices performed in the temple at Zarahemla. Indeed, he "confined himself wholly to the high priesthood of the holy order of God, to the testimony of the word, according to the spirit of revelation and prophecy" (Alma 4:20). This decision marked an important moment in Nephite history as he saw that there was "no way that he might reclaim them save it were in bearing down in pure testimony against them" (Alma 4:19). In so doing, he embodied the spirit of the next hundred years in Nephite history. He set the tone that allowed the righteous among them to prepare for the promised coming of the Messiah.

Alma's delivery of Alma 5 must have been stunning. It certainly was memorable. He spoke with strength, but also humility, and that delivery of eternal truths instills utmost confidence to this day. His words were traditionally familiar, often echoing the words of King Benjamin, while at the same time asking penetrating questions that were stunningly new. His sincere pleadings with his people were unmistakably clear and profoundly in touch with theology, ethics, and real life. We today can still reflect on this timeless speech and Alma's dedicated labors among the people in the land of Zarahemla as we ponder about our own spiritual growth, development, and standing before the Lord.

One may wonder and indeed some have asked questions about the possible sources of Alma the Elder's priesthood authority. But Alma's line of authority was never called into question within the Book of Mormon. He was a direct descendant of Nephi and, as such, would have been in a traditional position to have received and held priesthood authority.[19]

Some readers have speculated as to the nature and origin of Alma the Elder's priesthood authority because of his somewhat unorthodox "self-baptism" that occurred in conjunction with the baptism of Helam.[20] President Joseph Fielding Smith definitively stated:

> We may conclude that Alma held the priesthood before he, with others, became disturbed with King Noah. Whether this is so or not makes no difference because in the Book of Mormon it is stated definitely that he had authority.
>
> "And when he had said these words, the Spirit of the Lord was upon him, and he said: Helam, I baptize thee, *having authority from the Almighty God*" [Mosiah 18:13]. . . .

19   See Hugh Nibley, *Teachings of the Book of Mormon, Semester 2 Transcripts* (Provo, Utah: FARMS, 1993), 113.
20   See Mosiah 18:14.

If he had authority to baptize that is evidence that he had been baptized. Therefore, when Alma baptized himself with Helam that was not a case of Alma baptizing himself, but merely a token to the Lord of his humility and full repentance.[21]

Alma clearly communicates that shortly before the death of Alma the Elder—who served as the Nephite high priest—he did confer and consecrate the office of high priest upon his son, giving him "charge concerning all the affairs of the church" (Mosiah 29:42). The word *consecrate* is "the rendering of several Hebrew and Greek words" that mean "setting apart any thing or person to the worship or service of God."[22]

Alma, then, clearly had authority from God to serve the Nephites as high priest. He spoke with the voice of authority, and he acted boldly under divine inspiration. His words were long remembered. His priesthood lineage extended through his descendants Helaman[23] (who led the stripling warriors), and his son Helaman,[24] to his son Nephi (the great missionary to the Lamanites),[25] to that Nephi's son also called Nephi (who is the one who becomes the chief disciple of the resurrected Lord Jesus Christ),[26] and finally to Nephi (during the golden age in 4 Nephi), Amos, his son Amos, and his brother Ammaron,[27] the last of whom entrusted the records to Mormon.[28] In many ways, the Book of Mormon is a family history of the heritage of the priest Alma, who was converted by Abinadi, and the high priest Alma the Younger, whose authoritative words were especially preserved, remembered, and included as the wellsprings of righteousness in the Book of Mormon.

ALMA'S FIFTY QUESTIONS

Alma's speech to the Nephites at Zarahemla distinctively builds on fifty *rhetorical* questions—questions that are asked to create a dramatic effect and to make a point rather than to deliver or expect an immediate answer. Alma, of course, *did* expect the people to answer, but he wanted them to ponder personally

---

21   Joseph Fielding Smith, *Answers to Gospel Questions*, comp. Joseph Fielding Smith Jr. [1960] (Salt Lake City: Deseret Book, 2012), 3:53; emphasis added. In addition, in Jewish practice, immersion for ritual purification was typically self-administered.

22   Merrill F. Unger, "Consecration," in *The New Unger's Bible Dictionary*, rev. ed. (Chicago: The Moody Bible Institute of Chicago, 1960), 219.

23   See Alma 36–63.

24   See Helaman 1–5.

25   See Helaman 5–11.

26   See 3 Nephi 1–28.

27   See 4 Nephi 1:21, 47.

28   See Mormon 1:2–5.

and to answer inwardly—to ask themselves, *What about me?* He wanted to bring his listeners into the process, to cause them to think about their own lives, to ask questions that would help them receive personal revelation, act for themselves, and thus be held accountable.

He wanted to do the same for us.

Alma did not simply stand up in front of his audience and give them a list of things to do and ways in which they needed to improve. Nor did he answer all the questions he asked. He wisely left many of them open-ended, leaving his listeners responsible for finding the answers. Clearly, he wanted them—and us—to reflect deeply. Sister Wendy Watson Nelson said this about the power of such reflection:

> A wise Chilean biologist defined the term "reflection" [as] "The moment of reflection . . . is the moment when we become aware of that part of ourselves which we cannot see in any other way." . . . Alma invites us to look at our lives through the mirror of the Lord—the most important mirror of all. Alma invites us to reflect upon our standing before the Lord and increase our desire to change and to be better—all through the use of great questions.[29]

With his questions, Alma invites listeners, then and now, to reflect, to be introspective, to repent, and to recognize what they need to do so the blood of Christ can purify and cleanse them. He wants, as Sister Nelson has put it, to help his listeners see their lives by seeing themselves as mirroring and reflecting the life and goodness of the Lord or to stand before Him knowing that the Lord sees them as they really are, and we will too at that moment of reckoning. By going through that exercise, we will have a great desire to have "the image of God engraven upon [our] countenances" (Alma 5:19).

Whatever the manner of delivery, Alma's fifty questions defined the covenant renewal pattern, established the essential logic of the gospel, offered the choice of identifying with the fold of Christ or the fold of the devil, offered the challenge to repent, and testified to the reality of personal revelation. Through it all, he encouraged his listeners to actively prepare to meet God.

Although Alma's discourse was delivered in Zarahemla more than two thousand years ago, it was recorded and preserved for us in our day. We are as accountable and responsible as were those who heard him then. Alma's fifty

---

29   Wendy Watson Nelson, *Change Your Questions, Change Your Life* (Salt Lake City: Deseret Book, 2009), 6–7.

questions will help us make the mighty change. They will help us evaluate our present situation and determine the things we need to improve on. They will help us stay on the covenant path. As we apply the answers to our lives, they will deepen our conversion to the Lord Jesus Christ and His gospel. They will bring us nearer to God the Father, a primary purpose of the Book of Mormon. For in the sixth paragraph of the introduction to the Book of Mormon, we are told, "Concerning this record the Prophet Joseph Smith said: 'I told the brethren that the Book of Mormon was the most correct of any book on earth, and the keystone of our religion, and a man would get nearer to God by abiding by its precepts, than by any other book.'"

These questions closely resemble another address offered by Joshua, who concluded, "And if it seem evil unto you to serve the Lord, choose you this day whom ye will serve; . . . but as for me and my house, we will serve the Lord" (Joshua 24:15), and indeed this same covenant-renewing declaration is repeated at the beginning of the chapter later in Alma's life dealing with Korihor (see Alma 30:8–10). Like Joshua, Alma was always pressing his people—including us—to choose as their leader the good and true shepherd.

Alma's fifty rhetorical questions—questions that invite deep pondering—were inspired by the Holy Ghost and serve as a powerful tool for self-examination. His questions create an interactive tone, inspiring in us the desire to stand up and answer him. In fact, this interactive tone was characteristic of Hebrew oral poetry, which, in turn, was characteristic of festival discourse. While Alma's questions are indeed rhetorical, a dialogue often occurred between the speaker and his audience in Hebrew tradition: "In general it can be assumed that the audience were not mere passive spectators, but joined in actively, perhaps even by a certain amount of their own improvisation. Of such activities we can gain a few hints. *Refrains* and *questions* show that the people listening were not mute."[30] Even as Alma's audience in Zarahemla may have ritually responded to questions, we too can respond as we engrave our answers upon our hearts.

Though Alma's audience in Zarahemla struggled mightily as he stood before them, his words and the feelings of his heart had a profound effect. There was, after all, a happy ending. As Alma told the Gideonites about his audience in Zarahemla,

> But blessed be the name of God, that he hath given me to know,
> yea, hath given unto me the exceedingly great joy of knowing
> that they are established again in the way of his righteousness.

30   Wilfred G. E. Watson, *Classical Hebrew Poetry: A Guide to Its Techniques* (Sheffield, England: Journal for the Study of the Old Testament Press, 2009), 78.

> And I trust, according to the Spirit of God which is in me,
> that I shall also have joy over you; nevertheless I do not desire
> that my joy over you should come by the cause of so much
> afflictions and sorrow which I have had for the brethren at
> Zarahemla, for behold, my joy cometh over them after wading
> through much affliction and sorrow. (Alma 7:4–5)

Alma wants the same for us. He tells us that our names can be written in
the Lamb's Book of Life. He pleads with us to repent—not as a harsh judge,
but as one filled with love toward us. He gives us a wonderful promise at the
end: that Christ is there, that He is our shepherd, and that if we turn to Him,
we can be forgiven and live with Him and our Father forever.

The real test for us personally goes beyond that of just obtaining a testimony.
"It does not come down to just knowing the Book of Mormon is true, but [also]
whether we are true to the Book of Mormon. In the final analysis it is not if we
have digested" and absorbed each and every teaching in the Book of Mormon
but, rather, whether the Book of Mormon has enveloped and refined us.
"Therein lies the test" and the joy of passing that test. As Lehi said, "Men are,
that they *might* have joy," and they obtain that joy by freely choosing "liberty
and eternal life, through the great Mediator of all men" and not "captivity and
death, according to the captivity and power of the devil; for he seeketh that all
men might be miserable" (2 Nephi 2:25–27; emphasis added). Alma called this
process "the great plan of happiness" (Alma 42:8,16), and he hoped, above all,
that people would find that happiness by enjoying the love of God and enjoying
the life of righteousness by welcoming and embracing the true and candid
teachings of his greatest speech, found in Alma 5. That joyous process becomes
fully realized when we "can stand before the Lord as a living witness to the power
of the Book of Mormon in aiding [us] and attain 'the measure of the stature of
the fulness of Christ' (Ephesians 4:13)."[31]

Remember that the Lord has counseled us to hearken to the prophets.
This includes Alma and President Nelson! These are not casual statements but
reminders from the Lord and Mormon (see D&C 1:38; 21:4–6).

> And it came to pass that when Jesus had spoken these words unto
> Nephi, and to those who had been called, (now the number of
> them who had been called, and received power and authority
> to baptize, was twelve) and behold, he stretched forth his hand
> unto the multitude, and cried unto them, saying: Blessed are

---

31   Jack Christianson and K. Douglas Bassett, *Life Lessons from the Book of Mormon* (Springville, UT: Cedar
      Fort, 2007), 267–268.

ye if ye shall give heed unto the words of these twelve whom I have chosen from among you to minister unto you, and to be your servants; and unto them I have given power that they may baptize you with water; and after that ye are baptized with water, behold, I will baptize you with fire and with the Holy Ghost; therefore blessed are ye if ye shall believe in me and be baptized, after that ye have seen me and know that I am.

And again, more blessed are they who shall believe in your words because that ye shall testify that ye have seen me, and that ye know that I am. Yea, blessed are they who shall believe in your words, and come down into the depths of humility and be baptized, for they shall be visited with fire. (3 Nephi 12:1–2)

And wo be unto him that will not hearken unto the words of Jesus, and also to them whom he hath chosen and sent among them; for whoso receiveth not the words of Jesus and the words of those whom he hath sent receiveth not him; and therefore he will not receive them at the last day;

And it would be better for them if they had not been born. For do ye suppose that ye can get rid of the justice of an offended God, who hath been trampled under feet of men, that thereby salvation might come? (3 Nephi 28:34–35)

Prophets are the messengers of the Lord. They beckon us to repent and be faithful to our covenants. Alma's great sermon stands as a beacon to keep us on the covenant path and deepen our conversion.

THE 50 QUESTIONS OF ALMA 5

In this major discourse, Alma the Younger asks his people of the Church in Zarahemla fifty instructive and soul-searching questions. This chart lists all of these questions in overview, grouping them in the order in which they appear in Alma 5. These fifty questions are useful to all people who wish to assess their own personal conversion and improve their devoted standing before God.

- **Remembering God's Acts for His People**
First, Alma asks five questions about people needing to remember their own heritage and God's deliverance of their ancestors. Just as the Nephites were admonished to remember God's deliverance of their ancestors, so Latter-day Saints should remember their pioneer ancestors whenever and wherever they

lived and made sacrifices in building the kingdom of God. Remembering how merciful the Lord has been is a first step in being able to receive manifestations from the Holy Ghost of the truth of all things (Moroni 10:3).

1. Have you sufficiently retained in remembrance the captivity of your fathers? (v. 6)
2. Have you sufficiently retained in remembrance God's mercy and long-suffering towards your fathers? (v. 6)
3. Have you sufficiently retained in remembrance that he has delivered their souls from hell? (v. 6)
4. Were your fathers destroyed? (v. 8)
5. Were the bands of death broken, and the chains of hell which encircled your fathers about, were they loosed? (v. 9)

- **Knowing the Essential Logic of the Gospel**
Next, Alma invites people to ponder the conditions of salvation and the need to believe the prophets of God.

6. On what conditions were your fathers saved? (v. 10)
7. On what grounds had they to hope for salvation? (v. 10)
8. What is the cause of your fathers' being loosed from the bands of death, yea, and also the chains of hell? (v. 10)
9. Did not my father Alma believe in the words which were delivered by the mouth of Abinadi? (v. 11)
10. Was Abinadi not a holy prophet? (v. 11)
11. Did Abinadi not speak the words of God? (v. 11)
12. Did my father Alma believe them? (v. 11)

- **Being Personally Converted**
Third, he asks penetrating questions about each listener's repentance, change, faith, and hope. Still today, most of these questions invite a clear yes or no answer.

13. Have you spiritually been born of God? (v. 14)
14. Have you received His image in your countenance? (v. 14)
15. Have you experienced this mighty change in your heart? (v. 14)
16. Do you exercise faith in the redemption of Him who created you? (v. 15)
17. Do you look forward with an eye of faith? (v. 15)

- **Imagining the Judgment Day**
A dozen questions concern the state of the individual's soul at the final judgment day. Alma wishes to impress upon his audience that there are ultimately only two possible outcomes at the final judgment: eternal joy or eternal remorse.

Those who are righteous will have the image of God upon their countenances and will be found spotless and pure; others will be stained and unfit to abide the presence of God. The vivid belief that all people will someday stand before God to give an accounting and to be judged is a powerful motivator of moral behavior and spiritual growth.

18. Do you view this mortal body raised in immortality, and this corruption raised in incorruption, to stand before God to be judged according to the deeds which have been done in the mortal body? (v. 15)

19. Can you imagine to yourself that you hear the voice of the Lord, saying unto you, in that day: Come unto me you blessed, for behold your works have been works of righteousness upon the face of the earth? (v. 16)

20. Or do you imagine to yourself that you can lie unto the Lord in that day, and say—Lord, my works have been righteous works upon the face of the earth—and that he will save you? (v. 17)

21. Or otherwise, can you imagine yourself brought before the tribunal of God with your soul filled with guilt and remorse, having a remembrance of all your guilt, yea, a perfect remembrance of all your wickedness, yea, a remembrance that you have set at defiance the commandments of God? (v. 18)

22. Can you look up to God at that day with a pure heart and clean hands? (v. 19)

23. Can you look up, having the image of God engraven upon your countenance? (v. 19)

24. Can you think of being saved when you have yielded yourself to become subject to the devil? (v. 20)

25. How will you feel if you shall stand before the bar of God, having your garments stained with blood and all manner of filthiness? (v. 22)

26. What will these things testify against you? (v. 22)

27. Will they not testify that you are a murderer? (v. 23)

28. Will they not also testify that you are guilty of all manner of wickedness? (v. 23)

29. Do you suppose that such an one can have a place to sit down in the kingdom of God, with Abraham, with Isaac, and with Jacob, and also all the holy prophets, whose garments are cleansed and are spotless, pure and white? (v. 24)

- **Self-assessing One's Spiritual Condition**

The next seven questions probe the point that because experiencing a change of heart can be temporary, one must continually strive to be blameless before God.

30. If you have experienced a change of heart, and if you have felt to sing the song of redeeming love, can you feel so now? (v. 26)
31. Have you walked, keeping yourself blameless before God? (v. 27)
32. Could you say, if you were called to die at this time, within yourself, that you have been sufficiently humble? (v. 27)
33. Could you say that your garments have been cleansed and made white through the blood of Christ? (v. 27)
34. Are you stripped of pride? (v. 28)
35. Is there one among you who is not stripped of envy? (v. 29)
36. Is there one among you that doth make a mock of his brother, or that heapeth upon him persecutions? (v. 30)

• **Identifying with One "Fold" or the Other**
In Alma's view, those who are blameless are of the fold of God, and all others are of the fold of the devil.

37. If you are not the sheep of the good shepherd, of what fold are you? (v. 39)
38. The devil is your shepherd, and you are of his fold; and now, who can deny this? (v. 39)

• **Obtaining Spiritual Knowledge**
In this part of his speech, Alma guides the spiritual progress of his listeners by directing them in assessing their own spiritual condition, identifying with a community that believes in Jesus Christ, and personally obtaining spiritual knowledge.

39. Do you not suppose that I know of these things myself? (v. 45)
40. How do you suppose that I know of their surety? (v. 45)

• **Having No Reason to Refuse to Repent**
The last ten questions that Alma rhetorically asks the people of Zarahemla are all about refusing to repent of sins. Alma's phrase "trample the Holy One under your feet" (Alma 5:53) poignantly illustrates that individuals blatantly mock God when they know the source of their salvation and yet refuse to repent and partake of that gift. By ending his speech with these ten questions, Alma places the burden of repentance directly on the shoulders of each person who seeks to live a life pleasing to God.

41. Can you withstand these sayings? (v. 53)
42. Can you lay aside these things and trample the Holy One under your feet? (v. 53)
43. Can you be puffed up in the pride of your heart? (v. 53)

44. Will you still persist in the wearing of costly apparel and setting your heart upon the vain things of the world, upon your riches? (v. 53)

45. Will you persist in supposing that you are better than another? (v. 54)

46. Will you persist in the persecution of your brethren, who humble themselves and do walk after the holy order of God, wherewith they have been brought into this church having been sanctified by the Holy Spirit, and they do bring forth works which are meet for repentance? (v. 54)

47. Will you persist in turning your back upon the poor and the needy, and in withholding your substance from them? (v. 55)

48. The names of the righteous shall be written in the book of life, and unto them will I grant an inheritance at my right hand. What have you to say against this? (v. 58)

49. What shepherd is there having many sheep doth not watch over them, that the wolves enter not and devour his flock? (v. 59)

50. If a wolf enter his flock doth the shepherd not drive him out? (v. 59)

Without any answers, Alma concludes this speech with the following invitation. As he always did, Alma reaches out to encourage people to hearken to the words of the Lord, to seek to keep the commandments, and to partake of the fruit of the tree of life.

> And now I say unto you that the good shepherd doth call after you; and if you will hearken unto his voice he will bring you into his fold, and ye are his sheep; and he commandeth you that ye suffer no ravenous wolf to enter among you, that ye may not be destroyed. And now I, Alma, do command you in the language of him who hath commanded me, that ye observe to do the words which I have spoken unto you. I speak by way of command unto you that belong to the church; and unto those who do not belong to the church I speak by way of invitation, saying: Come and be baptized unto repentance, that ye also may be partakers of the fruit of the tree of life. (Alma 5:60–62)[32]

---

32   John W. and J. Gregory Welch, *Charting the Book of Mormon* (Provo: FARMS, 1999), charts 61–65.

CHAPTER TWO
BECOMING PERSONALLY CONVERTED

And now behold, I ask of you, my brethren of the church, have ye spiritually been born of God? (Alma 5:14)

OF THE LIFE-ALTERING QUESTIONS POSED by Alma, those touching on three specific topics seem particularly connected: repentance, conversion, and a mighty change of heart. As we ponder repentance, conversion, and a mighty change of heart, we are led to ask questions of our own: Which comes first in this mighty trifecta? Do we repent because we have been converted, or do we become converted as a result of repentance? Are we converted because we experience a mighty change of heart, or does a mighty change of heart follow conversion?

These soul-stirring questions and many others like them have been asked and thoughtfully addressed by many Latter-day Saints, especially Church leaders, as they have reflected on Alma's teachings in Alma 5. During the years since the publication of the Book of Mormon, this chapter has been cited 394 times, more often than any of Alma's other speeches.[1] Statements by these modern-day priesthood authorities capture the essence of Alma's high-priestly admonitions, especially concerning the spiritual process of repentance,

> **ALMA'S QUESTIONS ON CONVERSION**
>
> Have you spiritually been born of God? (See Alma 5:14)
>
> Have you received His image in your countenance? (See Alma 5:14)

---

1   Alma 5 has been cited in general conferences alone some 394 times (see https://scriptures.byu.edu/#::c0d5), with Alma 32–33 in developing faith in Christ as the next closest speech of Alma with a combined 259 citations.

conversion, and true renewal of the heart. Indeed, quotations of Alma 5:12–14, dealing with the "mighty change of heart," account for 93 such citations.

President Marion G. Romney, for example, described how the whole process of becoming personally converted works, adding to the mix of repentance, conversion, and mighty change the factors of obedience and the Holy Ghost—through Whom, of course, all take place:

> Conversion is effected by divine forgiveness, which remits sins. The sequence is something like this. An honest seeker hears the message. He asks the Lord in prayer if it is true. The Holy Spirit gives him a witness. This is a testimony. If one's testimony is strong enough, he repents and obeys the commandments. By such obedience he receives divine forgiveness which remits sin. Thus he is converted to a newness of life. His spirit is healed.[2]

Our prophet, President Russell M. Nelson, clearly illustrated how these principles are related, "Conversion means 'to turn with.' Conversion is a turning from the ways of the world to, and staying with, the ways of the Lord. Conversion includes repentance and obedience. Conversion brings a mighty change of heart."[3]

How does conversion take place? Elder David A. Bednar reminded us that "Samuel the Lamanite identified five basic elements in becoming converted unto the Lord: (1) believing in the teachings and prophecies of the holy prophets as they are recorded in the scriptures, (2) exercising faith in the Lord Jesus Christ, (3) repenting, (4) experiencing a mighty change of heart, and (5) 'becoming firm and steadfast in the faith.'[4] This is the pattern that leads to conversion."[5]

In determining how to structure this book, we carefully considered the sequence in which repentance, conversion, and a mighty change of heart take place. Through prayerful introspection, we arrived at the realization that while all three are essential, they may be experienced somewhat differently by each person who goes through this refining process. As a result, we decided to start with conversion, the process by which we abandon the things of the world and turn toward the things of the Lord. We follow that with the experience of a mighty change of heart, and later discuss the supernal doctrine of repentance, for it is something that should occur every day throughout our lives.

2   Marion G. Romney, in Conference Report, Oct. 1963, 24.
3   Russell M. Nelson, "Jesus Christ—the Master Healer," *Ensign* or *Liahona*, Nov. 2005, 85.
4   See Helaman 15:7–8.
5   David A. Bednar, "Converted unto the Lord," *Ensign* or *Liahona*, Nov. 2012.

As we consider conversion, which is the dominant theme of Alma 5, we do well to consider how many times in his seminal speech Alma may have been alluding to his own conversion experience, which he described initially in Mosiah 27 and then repeated more fully in Alma 36 and 38.[6] Alma does not face his audiences—then or now—and directly say, "You'd better believe what I'm saying, because here's what happened to me." We know, though, that he can speak with conviction because he had been there—had gone through the process of conversion in a way that few others experience. He knows what he's talking about.

Since Alma had repeatedly spoken of his remarkable conversion previous to this speech, his audience, gathered to hear him speak in Zarahemla, would have known the validity, genuineness, and sincerity of his questions.

Alma, as we remember, was "a very wicked and idolatrous man" who was "numbered among the unbelievers" (Mosiah 27:8). As he led many people away from the truth, he greatly hindered "the prosperity of the church of God; stealing away the hearts of the people; causing much dissension among the people; giving a chance for the enemy of God to exercise his power over them" (Mosiah 27:9).

We know that his father, Alma, had been praying with mighty faith that his rebellious son might be led to a knowledge of the truth. We know, too, that the Lord answers the faithful prayers of the righteous. The father's cries were not in vain, and there followed that amazing event experienced by Alma and the sons of Mosiah:

> behold, the angel of the Lord appeared unto them; and he descended as it were in a cloud; and he spake as it were with a voice of thunder, which caused the earth to shake upon which they stood;
>
> And so great was their astonishment, that they fell to the earth, and understood not the words which he spake unto them.
>
> Nevertheless he cried again, saying: Alma, arise and stand forth, for why persecutest thou the church of God? For the Lord hath said: This is my church, and I will establish it; and

---

6   See charts 106—"Three Accounts of Alma's Conversion"—and 107—"Shared Words in the Three Accounts of Alma's Conversion"—in John W. and J. Gregory Welch, *Charting the Book of Mormon* (Provo, Utah: FARMS, 1999). See also S. Kent Brown, "Alma's Conversion: Reminiscences in His Sermons," in *The Book of Mormon: Alma, The Testimony of the Word*, eds. Monte S. Nyman and Charles D. Tate Jr. (Provo: BYU Religious Studies Center, 1991), discussing the appearances of elements in Alma's conversion narrative throughout all of Alma's speeches.

nothing shall overthrow it, save it is the transgression of my
people. (Mosiah 27:11–13)

Verifying that he had been sent from God, the angel of the Lord told Alma
to go his way and seek no more to destroy the Church—and that if Alma
persisted in his evil, he would be "cast off" (Mosiah 27:16). It seems likely that
this sobering exposition of the consequences of his evil actions would have been
on Alma's mind as he later told his listeners about standing before God at the
judgment bar.

Imagining ourselves in such a position, it is easy to understand what
happened next:

> And now Alma and those that were with him fell again to the
> earth, for great was their astonishment; for with their own
> eyes they had beheld an angel of the Lord; and his voice was as
> thunder, which shook the earth; and they knew that there was
> nothing save the power of God that could shake the earth and
> cause it to tremble as though it would part asunder.
>
> And now the astonishment of Alma was so great that he
> became dumb, that he could not open his mouth; yea, and he
> became weak, even that he could not move his hands; therefore
> he was taken by those that were with him, and carried helpless,
> even until he was laid before his father. (Mosiah 27:18–19)

Upon seeing his lame and dumb son, Alma's father rejoiced. He recognized
prayers answered. He and his priests fasted and prayed that Alma might be
able to open his mouth and that his limbs would be strengthened—not so
much for Alma's sake, but "that the eyes of the people might be opened to
see and know of the goodness and glory of God" (Mosiah 27:22). Three days
after seeing the angel, Alma stood and spoke with conviction, saying, "I have
repented of my sins, and have been redeemed of the Lord; behold I am born
of the Spirit" (Mosiah 27:24).

As Alma addressed the Nephites at Zarahemla in Alma 5, he spoke with power
about becoming converted, experiencing a mighty change of heart, coming to an
awful recollection of all our sins, repenting, choosing which shepherd to follow,
and preparing to meet God. The power with which he spoke and the fervor with
which he delivered his message were born of his own experience. All who heard
his words—then and now—could reasonably conclude, "Alma knows what he's
talking about, and I really ought to listen and take this to heart."

WHAT IS *CONVERSION?*

When we hear the word *conversion*, we often think of those we call "converts"—those who, usually as adults, find and accept the gospel and become baptized. We fail to remember that every member of the Church, no matter when baptized, must also become converted, else their testimony will be hollow. President M. Russell Ballard teaches, "We often think of conversion as applying only to investigators, but there are some members who are not yet fully converted and who have yet to experience the mighty change of heart described in the scriptures."[7]

Yes, those who accept the gospel and the invitation to be baptized are on the way to conversion. In the full gospel sense, wrote Elder Bruce R. McConkie,

> *Conversion* is more—far more—than merely changing one's belief from that which is false to that which is true; it is more than the acceptance of the verity of gospel truths, than acquiring a testimony. To convert is to change from one status to another, and gospel conversion consists in the transformation of man from his fallen and carnal state to a state of saintliness. A convert is one who . . . has been born again; where once he was spiritually dead, he has been regenerated to a state of spiritual life. . . . He changes his whole way of life, and the nature and structure of his very being is quickened and changed by the power of the Holy Ghost.[8]

Convert is a verb—an action word. To convert cannot be a passive act. The verb *convert* means "to turn from one belief or course to another." Interestingly, the Hebrew word for *repent* is literally "to turn," meaning to turn away from unrighteousness and to turn, or to return, unto the Lord. The word *conversion* likewise means "a spiritual and moral change attending a change of belief with conviction." President Marion G. Romney provided insight into the circumstances of true conversion. As used in scripture, President Romney said, *conversion*

> generally implies not merely mental acceptance of Jesus and his teachings, but also a motivating faith in him and in his gospel, a faith which works a transformation, an actual change in one's understanding of life's meaning and in one's allegiance to God—

---

7   M. Russell Ballard, "Now Is the Time," *Ensign*, Nov. 2000.

8   Bruce R. McConkie, *Mormon Doctrine*, 2nd ed. (Salt Lake City: Bookcraft, 1966), 162.

in interest, in thought, and in conduct. While conversion may be accomplished in stages, one is not really converted in the full sense of the term unless and until he is at heart a new person.[9]

Those who are truly converted will be changed by Christ; as a result, taught President Ezra Taft Benson,[10] they will be captained by Christ. Those captained by Christ want to "walk, even as he walked" (1 John 2:6). As the Apostle Peter said, they will "follow his steps" (1 Peter 2:21). Their will is swallowed up in His will,[11] and they earnestly seek what the Lord would have them do.[12]

As President Harold B. Lee wrote, those captained by Christ "set a fire in others because they themselves are on fire."[13] "Men and women captained by Christ will be consumed in Christ. . . . Not only would they die for the Lord, but, more important, they want to live for Him."[14]

That kind of fire, that kind of devotion, is the hallmark of conversion.

BEING BORN AGAIN

Alma told his listeners that all of them and all of us—"old and young, both bond and free; yea, I say unto you the aged, and also middle aged and the rising generation"—must "repent and be born again" (Alma 5:49).

At first glance, the phrase *born again* seems odd—and taken literally, it is impossible. That same thought occurred to a Pharisee named Nicodemus, who came to visit the Savior one night under the cloak of darkness, desiring to be taught by Jesus but anxious to avoid being seen by any of his peers. As the Gospel of John tells it, the first thing the Savior told Nicodemus was, "Except a man be born again, he cannot see the kingdom of God" (John 3:3).

Nicodemus, naturally confused by Christ's pronouncement, asked, "How can a man be born when he is old? can he enter the second time into his mother's womb, and be born?" (John 3:4).

The phrase *born again* is much more familiar to us than it was to Nicodemus, and so most of us probably have a fairly clear sense of what it means to "be born of water and of the Spirit" (John 3:5).

Part of being "born again" involves being baptized (born of water) and receiving the Holy Ghost (born of the Spirit), both of which purge our sins. The

9   Marion G. Romney, in Conference Report, Oct. 1975, 107–108.
10   See Ezra Taft Benson, "Born of God," *Ensign*, Oct. 1989.
11   See John 5:30.
12   See Acts 9:6.
13   Harold B. Lee, "Stand Ye in Holy Places," *Ensign*, May 1974, 192.
14   Ezra Taft Benson, "Born of God," *Ensign*, Oct. 1989.

ordinances involved are essential, according to the Prophet Joseph Smith, who taught that being born again "comes by the Spirit of God through ordinances."[15]

But the process of being born extends much further. Being born again consists of coming alive to the things of the Spirit and of righteousness. In an address delivered on July 11, 1956, Elder Mark E. Petersen described the rebirth process this way:

> That birth of the spirit means something more than most of us normally realize. Through proper teaching, a conviction is born in our soul. Faith develops. Through it we see how important it is to become like Christ. We see ourselves as we are in contrast to a Christ-like soul. A desire for a change-over is born within us. The change-over begins. We call it repentance. Through our faith and as part of our conversion or change from one state to another, we begin to see sin in its true light. . . . We strive with all our souls to become like the Savior.[16]

Conversion is the process of being born of God. *Born of God* or *born again* refers to the personal spiritual experience through which we receive a forgiveness of sins and a witness from God that if we continue to live the commandments and endure to the end, we will inherit eternal life. The scriptures teach that just as each of us is "born into the world by water, and blood, and the spirit," so must we be "born again" of water and the Spirit and be cleansed by the blood of Christ.[17] To be born of God implies a sanctifying process by which we are made pure and holy so that we can enjoy the companionship of the Holy Ghost. When we are born again, we are spiritually begotten sons and daughters of God and more specifically of Jesus Christ.[18] Being born again is the process that fuels the inner transformation that Alma referred to in his address as a *mighty change of heart*.[19]

When Nicodemus approached the Savior under cover of darkness, he acknowledged that Christ was "a teacher come from God," saying, "for no man can do these miracles that thou doest, except God be with him" (John 3:2). From that perspective, Nicodemus naturally assumed at first that being "born again" would have involved an unparalleled, even absurd, miracle—

---

15   *Teachings of the Prophet Joseph Smith,* sel. Joseph Fielding Smith [1976], 162.

16   C. Max Caldwell, "A Mighty Change," in *The Book of Mormon: Alway, the Testimony of the Word,* ed. Monte S. Nyman and Charles D. Tate Jr. (Provo, UT: Religious Studies Center, Brigham Young University, 1992), 27–46.

17   See Moses 6:59; John 3:5.

18   See Mosiah 5:7; 27:25.

19   *Encyclopedia of Mormonism* [1992], "Born of God," 2:218.

that of a man somehow entering his mother's womb a second time and then going through the birth process again.

Nicodemus was wrong. That's not what the Savior was talking about. But Nicodemus was also right: the process of being born again is without doubt a miracle, just not the kind he first thought. Elder McConkie described for us what a true miracle it is to be born again:

> Perhaps the greatest miracle . . . is the healing of sin-sick souls so that those who are spiritually blind and deaf and diseased become again pure and clean and heirs of salvation. Perhaps the greatest miracle of all is that which happens in the life of each person who is born again; who receives the sanctifying power of the Holy Spirit of God in his life; who has sin and evil burned out of his soul as though by fire; who lives again spiritually.[20]

In his general conference address in April 2007, Elder David A. Bednar said that "one of the principal purposes of our mortal existence is to be spiritually changed and transformed through the Atonement of Jesus Christ." But he also explained that it is not an instant change, a sudden transformation. In discussing the mighty change that comes as a part of conversion, Elder Bednar said that conversion

> is mighty, not minor—a spiritual rebirth and fundamental change of what we feel and desire, what we think and do, and what we are. Indeed, the essence of the gospel of Jesus Christ entails a fundamental and permanent change in our very nature made possible through our reliance upon "the merits, and mercy, and grace of the Holy Messiah" (2 Nephi 2:8). As we choose to follow the Master, we choose to be changed—to be spiritually reborn. . . .
>
> Spiritual rebirth . . . typically does not occur quickly or all at once; it is an ongoing process—not a single event. Line upon line and precept upon precept, gradually and almost imperceptibly, our motives, our thoughts, our words, and our deeds become aligned with the will of God. This phase of the transformation process requires time, persistence, and patience. . . .[21]

---

20   Bruce R. McConkie, *The Mortal Messiah* (Salt Lake City: Deseret Book, 1981), 3:269.

21   David A. Bednar, "Ye Must Be Born Again," *Ensign* or *Liahona*, May 2007.

SPIRITUALLY BORN OF GOD: ASSESSING OUR SPIRITUAL CONDITION

Directing his comments to the Nephites in Zarahemla, primarily those wicked members of the Church and those present who did not belong to the Church, Alma asked, "And now behold, I ask of you, my brethren of the church, have ye spiritually been born of God?" (Alma 5:14).

Alma's remarks were reflective of the first words he spoke upon arising from the three-day ordeal that resulted in his great conversion:

> Marvel not that all mankind, yea, men and women, all nations, kindreds, tongues and people, must be born again; yea, born of God, changed from their carnal and fallen state, to a state of righteousness, being redeemed of God, becoming his sons and daughters;
>
> And thus they become new creatures; and unless they do this, they can in nowise inherit the kingdom of God. (Mosiah 27:25–26)

Alma's uniquely intense conversion experience highlighted the absolute necessity of spiritual rebirth. The difference between his pre-conversion life and his post-conversion life was so marked—from "the gall of bitterness" to "exquisite and sweet joy" (Alma 36:18, 20–21)—that he yearned for others to "taste of the exceeding joy of which [he] did taste" (Alma 36:24).

Everything good and valuable in Alma's life began when he was "born again." He attributed all his wisdom and eternal progress to that moment of spiritual rebirth: "Now, behold, I say unto you, if I had not been born of God I should not have known these things" (Alma 36:5).[22] In his corollary to the oft-cited maxim "Wickedness never was happiness" (Alma 41:10), Alma also attributed all true joy to spiritual rebirth: "All men that are in a state of nature . . . a carnal state, are in the gall of bitterness and in the bonds of iniquity . . . and they have gone contrary to the nature of God; therefore, *they are in a state contrary to the nature of happiness*" (Alma 41:11; emphasis added).

According to Alma, both mortal and eternal happiness require spiritual rebirth. Alma's emphasis on "a mighty change of heart" and being "born of God" springs from his own miraculous transformation. In fact, almost all references to being "born of God" in the Book of Mormon are made by Alma, either in Alma 5 or as he tells the story of his own conversion.[23]

---

22   See also Alma 38:6.

23   See Mosiah 27:25, 28; Alma 5:14; 36:5, 23, 24, 26; 38:6. The one exception is in the report of Aaron, one of the four sons of Mosiah, who was present when the angel instigated the conversion of Alma. The father of King Lamoni asked Aaron, "What shall I do that I may have this eternal life *of which thou hast spoken*? Yea, what shall I do that I maybe born of God?" (Alma 22:15; emphasis added).

RECEIVING CHRIST'S IMAGE IN OUR COUNTENANCE

After asking his listeners if they had spiritually been born of God, Alma immediately posed another intriguing question: "Have ye received his image in your countenances?" (Alma 5:14).

> An "image" is not just an outward visual impression but also a vivid representation, a graphic display, or a total likeness of something. It is a person or thing very much like another, a copy or counterpart. Likewise, countenance does not simply mean a facial expression or visual appearance. The word comes from an old French term originally denoting "behavior," "demeanor," or "conduct." In earlier times, the word countenance was used with these meanings in mind.
>
> Therefore, to receive Christ's image in one's countenance means to acquire the Savior's likeness in behavior, to be a copy or reflection of the Master's life. This is not possible without a mighty change in one's pattern of living. It requires, too, a change in feelings, attitudes, desires, and spiritual commitment.[24]

A few minutes later, Alma then asked his listeners, "Can you look up, having the image of God engraven upon your countenances?" (Alma 5:19).

Alma *almost* repeats the language of verse fourteen with this question, which seems very similar. But there is a significant difference between having "*received* his image in your countenances" and "having the image of God *engraven* upon your countenances." When we *receive* His image, we have accepted it as a way of life. But *engraven* has a much deeper meaning, connoting that the image of Christ is carved and inscribed in our very heart. It is embedded there for life, by the influences of righteous people around us, by the works of our own hands and choices, and above all by the knowledge and wisdom of the Lord Himself. And this great process of becoming like Christ is because He is the one helping us become like Him. He is the engraver. He is the One who perfects us.[25] Christ is the One through which we are able to make this great transformation.[26] As He said when He promised that He would never forget Zion, "I have graven thee upon the palms of my hands; thy walls are continually before me" (Isaiah 49:16).

The material significance of the word *engravened*, especially in the minds of a Nephite audience, which understood a fair amount about engraving

---

24 Andrew Skinner, "Alma's 'Pure Testimony' (Alma 5–8)," in *Book of Mormon, Part 1: 1 Nephi to Alma 29*, Studies in Scripture, Vol. 7, ed. Kent P. Jackson (Salt Lake City, UT: Deseret Book, 1987), 301.

25 See Moroni 10:32–33.

26 See Hebrews 13:21; Philippians 4:13.

on metal plates, was clearly articulated by David P. Parkinson at a Book of Mormon symposium held at Brigham Young University in 1982:

> It may, in fact, be possible to reflect to a degree the image of God upon our countenance, but Alma asks if His image is *engravened* upon our countenance. He doesn't say penciled in or drawn on or water colored; it can't be hastily scratched or even typed on; but the word *engraved* means impressed deeply well below the surface. We might think of how a metal plate is engraved upon with a stylus, a sharp engraving tool—deep, clean, gleaming characters or letters embedded forever into precious material or matter. . . .
>
> Proper engraving seems to require an instrument made of a harder substance than the matter upon which you are engraving. . . . Likewise, it seems that the Lord uses various processes and some very hard instruments to help engrave and impress upon us the more important things in life. . . .
>
> The instrument used to engrave the image of greatness and godliness upon us and our countenance may be the instrument of suffering or persecution or sacrifice or service and charity . . . Incredible but true, worthy Saints seem to stand in a position of having his attributes and his character traits gradually engraven upon us. As we begin to resemble him, we may, with him, stand as "one, the children of Christ, and heirs to the kingdom of God." (4 Nephi 1:17)[27]

What Alma is really asking—both his listeners then and we readers now—is how deep our conversion is. Are we rooted in Christ? Do we seek to act like, be like, and emulate Christ? Have we taken upon ourselves the divine nature of Christ?[28] This question is so important that Alma repeated it a second time, adding a deeper meaning and level of commitment to the Lord.

Receiving the Lord's image and having it engraved upon our countenance suggests a deeply symbolic meaning of becoming like our Savior Jesus Christ. Almost a century after Alma delivered his stirring speech, the Lord Himself spoke of the same thing while addressing the Nephites in Bountiful. To that

---

27 David P. Parkinson, "Engraving the Image of God upon Our Countenances," in *The Sixth Annual CES Religious Educators Symposium on the Book of Mormon* (Salt Lake City: The Church of Jesus Christ of Latter-day Saints, 1982), 70, 72.

28 See 2 Peter 1:3–10.

faithful group who had gathered to see their resurrected Savior, He asked a question followed by an invitation to become like Him when He said, "Therefore, what manner of men ought ye to be? Verily I say unto you, even as I am" (3 Nephi 27:27).

As we come to Christ and follow Him with full purpose of heart, we can become like Him.[29] In his final words before bidding readers of the Book of Mormon farewell, Moroni tells us how to engrave the Savior's image on our hearts so deeply that we become fully converted and perfected in Him:

> Yea, come unto Christ, and be perfected in him, and deny yourselves of all ungodliness; and if ye shall deny yourselves of all ungodliness, and love God with all your might, mind and strength, then is his grace sufficient for you, that by his grace ye may be perfect in Christ; and if by the grace of God ye are perfect in Christ, ye can in nowise deny the power of God.
>
> And again, if ye by the grace of God are perfect in Christ, and deny not his power, then are ye sanctified in Christ by the grace of God, through the shedding of the blood of Christ, which is in the covenant of the Father unto the remission of your sins, that ye become holy, without spot. (Moroni 10:32–33)

PERSONAL CONVERSION COMES THROUGH THE SPIRIT

True conversion consists in coming to a "knowledge of the truth" (Alma 23:6), something that occurs only through the Holy Spirit. To understand the power of the truth and the essential role of the Holy Ghost in testifying of the truth, we need only consider the missionary labors of the sons of Mosiah. As they journeyed many days in the wilderness, they "fasted much and prayed much that the Lord would grant unto them a portion of his Spirit to go with them, and abide with them," that they might bring the Lamanites "to the knowledge of the truth" (Alma 17:9). We know the result of that fasting and prayer:

> As many [of the Lamanites] as were brought to the knowledge of the truth, through the preaching of Ammon and his brethren, according to the spirit of revelation and of prophecy, and the power of God working miracles in them—yea, . . . as the Lord liveth, as many of the Lamanites as believed in their preaching, and were converted unto the Lord, never did fall away.

---

29   See Matthew 11:28–30; 3 Nephi 27:20; D&C 93:1.

For they became a righteous people; they did lay down the weapons of their rebellion, that they did not fight against God any more. . . .

Now, these are they who were converted unto the Lord. (Alma 23:6–8)

Elder Bednar taught it was the "powerful combination of both testimony and conversion that produced firmness and steadfastness and provided spiritual protection to the converted Lamanites:

> They never did fall away and surrendered "the weapons of their rebellion, that they did not fight against God any more." To set aside cherished "weapons of rebellion" such as selfishness, pride, and disobedience requires more than merely believing and knowing. Conviction, humility, repentance, and submissiveness precede the abandonment of our weapons of rebellion. Do you and I still possess weapons of rebellion that keep us from becoming converted unto the Lord? If so, then we need to repent now.[30]

It is by the power of the Holy Ghost that all of us come to a knowledge of the "truth of all things" (Moroni 10:5).[31] That knowledge of the truth, as revealed by the Holy Ghost, brings us to Christ and facilitates the conversion process. In fact, coming to the knowledge of the truth is the essence of conversion and making the mighty change. And it cannot happen without the Holy Ghost.

President Henry B. Eyring powerfully testified of the Holy Ghost's role in teaching us the truth:

> Just as the Holy Ghost strengthens us against evil, He also gives us the power to discern truth from falsehood. *The truth that matters most is verified only by revelation from God.* Our human reason and the use of our physical senses will not be enough. We live in a time when even the wisest will be hard-pressed to distinguish truth from clever deception. . . . While a member of the Quorum of the Twelve Apostles, George Q. Cannon urged that we make a constant quest for the Spirit to be with us. He promised, and I promise it as well, that if we pursue that course, we "will never lack for knowledge" of the truth, "never be in

---

30   David A. Bednar, "Converted unto the Lord," *Ensign* or *Liahona*, Nov. 2012.
31   See also John 15:26; 1 Corinthians 2:11–13; 2 Nephi 31:18; Alma 5:46; 3 Nephi 11:36.

doubt or in darkness," and our "faith will be strong, [our] joy
. . . full."[32]

Conversion comes only through the Spirit. Even though Alma saw an angel,
he still had to fast and pray to receive the confirmation of the Spirit before his
conversion was complete. The *angel* is not what caused the conversion. Many
others have seen wonders and angels without experiencing conversion (consider
as just one example the experiences of Laman and Lemuel). Conversion is
found in a change of heart, in having the image of Christ engraven in our
countenances and through the companionship of the Holy Ghost.[33]

For us, the testimony that accompanies conversion is the foundation of
complete faith and trust in God the Father and our Savior Jesus Christ. It will
help us always stay on the covenant path because we know "all things have
been done in the wisdom of him who knoweth all things" (2 Nephi 2:24). It is
no light thing to be able to bear witness of God the Father and of the atoning
sacrifice of His Son, Jesus Christ. To do so is evidence of our true conversion.

We can know all the great and miraculous things that God the Father
and our Savior Jesus Christ do by the power of the Holy Ghost[34] because the
Holy Ghost testifies of all truth.[35]

Remember again the mighty conversion experienced by the Lamanites when
they came to the knowledge of the truth: they "were converted unto the Lord"
and "never did fall away" (Alma 23:6).

The conversion of the Lamanites was powerful—but the same thing happens
in every conversion, including ours. Including yours. It is the Holy Spirit who
converts and testifies of all the truths of the gospel of Jesus Christ. And in the
end, knowing that Christ is real and that He suffered and died for us that we
might have eternal life is the knowledge that leads to true conversion.[36]

---

32   Henry B. Eyring, "The Holy Ghost as Your Companion," *Ensign* or *Liahona*, Nov. 2015; emphasis added.
33   See Alma 5:45–46.
34   See Acts 10:38.
35   See Moroni 10:5.
36   See Alma 23:5–6.

CHAPTER THREE

EXPERIENCING A MIGHTY CHANGE OF HEART

And now behold, I ask of you, my brethren of the church . . . Have ye received his image in your countenances? Have ye experienced this mighty change in your hearts? (Alma 5:14)

ELDER JOSEPH B. WIRTHLIN SAID, "Once faith grows into a firm, abiding testimony, giving us hope in our Heavenly Father's plan of happiness; once we see through the eye of faith that we are children of a loving Father who has given us the gift of His Son to redeem us, we experience a mighty change in our hearts."[1]

WHAT IS A "MIGHTY CHANGE OF HEART"?

Having a change of heart is all part of being born again and becoming a new creature.[2] It becomes a heart where the word of God and the Holy Spirit reside. The Apostle Paul refers to this change as having the "mind of Christ" (1 Corinthians 2:16).

This was the very change that the people of King Benjamin experienced:

> ### ALMA'S QUESTIONS ON A MIGHTY CHANGE OF HEART
>
> Have you spiritually been born of God? (See Alma 5:14)
>
> Have you received His image in your countenance? (See Alma 5:14)
>
> Have you experienced this mighty change in your hearts? (See Alma 5:14)
>
> If you have experienced a change of heart, and if you have felt to sing the song of redeeming love, can you feel so now? (See Alma 5:26)

---

1   Joseph B. Wirthlin, "Cultivating Divine Attributes," *Ensign*, Nov. 1998, 25.
2   See Mosiah 27:25–26.

> And they all cried with one voice, saying: Yea, we believe
> all the words which thou hast spoken unto us; and also, we
> know of their surety and truth, *because of the Spirit of the Lord*
> *Omnipotent, which has wrought a mighty change in us, or in our*
> *hearts, that we have no more disposition to do evil, but to do good*
> *continually.* (Mosiah 5:2; emphasis added)

When our hearts become changed, the inner person is changed. That change becomes who you are. The heart is the very spirit of the being.[3] In Proverbs we learn, "For as he thinketh in his heart, so is he" (Proverbs 23:7). A changed heart, then, is a changed person!

A mighty change of heart takes place in us because of our faith in the name of Christ[4] and by the power of the Holy Ghost.[5] It takes place as a result of full and sincere repentance. Elder Allen D. Haynie said, "Repentance is real and it works. It is not a fictional experience or the product 'of a frenzied mind.' It has the power to lift burdens and replace them with hope. It can lead to a mighty change of heart that results in our having 'no more disposition to do evil, but to do good continually.'"[6]

When we are in the process of making the mighty change, we will ask questions like, "What shall I do?" King Lamoni's father asked this question of Aaron and received the answer that provides powerful evidence of what a mighty change of heart looks like:

> And it came to pass that after Aaron had expounded these
> things unto him, the king said: What shall I do that I may
> have this eternal life of which thou hast spoken? Yea, what
> shall I do that I may be *born of God, having this wicked spirit*
> *rooted out of my breast, and receive his Spirit, that I may be*
> *filled with joy, that I may not be cast off at the last day?* Behold,
> said he, I will give up all that I possess, yea, I will forsake my
> kingdom, that I may receive this great joy.
>
> But Aaron said unto him: If thou desirest this thing, if
> thou wilt bow down before God, yea, *if thou wilt repent of all*
> *thy sins, and will bow down before God, and call on his name in*
> *faith, believing that ye shall receive,* then shalt thou receive the
> hope which thou desirest. (Alma 22:15–16; emphasis added)

---

3   See D&C 8:2–3.
4   See Mosiah 5:7.
5   See Mosiah 5:2; Moroni 8:26; Alma 5:45–46; 3 Nephi 27:20.
6   Allen D. Haynie, "Remembering in Whom We Have Trusted," *Ensign* or *Liahona*, Nov. 2015.

The purity that follows sincere repentance is clearly a significant part of a mighty change of heart. Those who experience a mighty change of heart, we are told, have no more disposition to do evil. After King Benjamin asked his people if they believed the words he had spoken to them, as we see in Mosiah 5:2, they affirmed that their belief "wrought a mighty change in us, or in our hearts, that we have no more disposition to do evil, but to do good continually" (Mosiah 5:2).

Of that declaration, Elder David A. Bednar said, "Accepting the words spoken, gaining a testimony of their truthfulness, and exercising faith in Christ produced a mighty change of heart and a firm determination to improve and become better."[7]

Elder Robert D. Hales similarly said,

> This change . . . is possible only through the Savior. Jesus promised: "If men come unto me I will show unto them their weakness. . . . And my grace is sufficient for all men that humble themselves before me; for if they humble themselves before me, and have faith in me, then will *I make weak things become strong unto them*" (Ether 12:27; emphasis added). As we are *made new* in Christ, our very natures change and we no longer want to go back to our old ways.

Elder Lowell D. Wood spoke of some of those "weak things" that need to change before we can experience a mighty change of heart, including "our worldly ways, our pride, and our selfishness." Then, as we "yield to the promptings of the Holy Ghost, we should experience a 'mighty change in [our] hearts' and become willing to submit to or accept 'all things which the Lord seeth fit to inflict upon [us].'"[8]

A mighty change of heart is characterized by having the Father's image in our countenances, our faces. Elder Theodore M. Burton observed that when we have such a mighty change of heart that we follow the Father and the Savior, we experience a change not only in our heart, but also in the way we *look*:

> If we truly accept God in our lives and live in accordance with his commandments, God will work a mighty change in our appearance and we will begin to appear more like our Heavenly Father, in whose image we have been created. Could it be this appearance we recognize when we meet men and women who are trying to live close to the Lord?[9]

7   David A. Bednar, "Converted unto the Lord," *Ensign* or *Liahona*, Nov. 2012.
8   Lowell D. Wood, "Come unto Christ," *Ensign*, May 1993, 88.
9   Theodore M. Burton, "The Need for Total Commitment," *Ensign*, Jan. 1974, 114.

In identifying what leads to a mighty change of heart, we would do well to study the life of Alma the Younger, whose experience is one of the most powerful examples of a mighty change of heart in all of scripture.[10] Alma was the son of Alma the Elder, who had been at the court of wicked King Noah when the Prophet Abinadi preached his ultimate sermon on repentance before being burned at the stake. The elder Alma fled with his righteous followers and eventually reached Zarahemla.

Like the sons of King Mosiah, Alma the Younger was initially "numbered among the unbelievers" (Mosiah 27:8) and "the very vilest of sinners" (Mosiah 28:4). But the Lord had an important calling for him and the sons of Mosiah. Sometime between 100 and 92 BC, a heavenly messenger intervened and brought about their spiritual transformation,[11] which is one of the most stirring episodes in all scripture.

As a result of that angelic visit, Alma and the sons of Mosiah redirected their lives in what could only be described as a mighty change of heart. Alma was subsequently appointed chief judge of the land (around 91 BC) and commenced his service by overcoming the forces of incipient priestcraft and defeating the conspirator Amlici, who had designed an overthrow of the government.

A few years later, Alma was consecrated high priest of the Church by his father.[12] Alma subsequently delegated his judgment seat office to another, that he "might go forth among his people, or among the people of Nephi, that he might preach the word of God unto them, to stir them up in remembrance of their duty" (Alma 4:19).

After reforming the Church in Zarahemla and preaching the gospel in other cities in the region, Alma was rejected outright in the city of Ammonihah and was forced to abandon his mission. An angel of the Lord intervened and commanded him to return to the city, so he returned "speedily" (Alma 8:18). There he met Amulek, whom the angel had commissioned to receive and house the traveling prophet. The two delivered powerful sermons on faith, repentance, and the Atonement to the hard-hearted citizens and warned them of the impending destruction of the city, but these missionaries were again rejected by the local leadership (including the lawyer Zeezrom for a time).

Alma and Amulek were constrained by the Spirit to remain silent during the martyrdom of many believers.[13] They were cast into prison to suffer for

10   The following information on Alma taken from Ed J. Pinegar and Richard J. Allen, *Book of Mormon Who's Who: A Comprehensive Guide to the People in the Book of Mormon* (American Fork, Utah: Covenant Communications, 2007), 12–13.
11   See Mosiah 27:11–18, Alma 36, and Alma 38. See charts 106 and 107 in Welch, *Charting the Book of Mormon*.
12   See Alma 4:4; 5:3.
13   Regarding those who were martyred, see Alma 14:11: "the Lord receiveth them up unto himself, in glory."

days until they were liberated through the power of God. Zeezrom, the leader who had initially participated in rejecting and persecuting Alma and Amulek, was converted and returned with them to Zarahemla.

Alma's ministry thereafter consists of an intense sequence of valiant achievements, including making arrangements for the safety and settlement of the righteous Lamanites who were converted by the sons of Mosiah,[14] confounding the sign-seeking, anti-Christ Korihor,[15] preaching powerfully in the regions round about,[16] and providing remarkable counsel and blessings for his sons.[17] Shortly thereafter, Alma set off for the land Melek but was never heard of again, presumably being translated after the manner of Moses.[18]

Alma, the tireless champion of faith who experienced such a mighty change of heart, is perhaps best remembered for the burning desire of his heart—to bring joy and truth to all of God's children:

> O that I were an angel, and could have the wish of mine heart, that I might go forth and speak with the trump of God, with a voice to shake the earth, and cry repentance unto every people!
>
> Yea, I would declare unto every soul, as with the voice of thunder, repentance and the plan of redemption, that they should repent and come unto our God, that there might not be more sorrow upon all the face of the earth. (Alma 29:1–2)

Of Alma, Elder Robert D. Hales said,

> Alma the Younger provides a vivid example in the account of his conversion. Alma had been rebellious, even so much that he and the sons of Mosiah went about "seeking to destroy the church of God" (Alma 36:6). Imagine the pain and heartache of Alma's parents and more importantly of Heavenly Father and Jesus, who finally sent an angel to tell him, "If thou wilt of thyself be destroyed, seek no more to destroy the church of God" (Alma 36:9). It was painful enough that Alma should choose disobedience, but he was also causing others to rebel against the word of God.[19]

---

14 See Alma 27–28.
15 See Alma 30.
16 See Alma 31.
17 See Alma 36–42.
18 See Alma 45:18–19.
19 Robert D. Hales, "Healing Soul and Body," *Ensign*, Nov. 1998.

Alma provided a vivid description of his feelings after his mighty change of heart when he remembered his sins. Alma said he "was tormented with the pains of hell" (Alma 36:13) and "was racked with eternal torment" (Alma 36:12) as he remembered his disobedience and rebellion against God. Consider the change in Alma's feelings after he had experienced a mighty change of heart and had turned to God: "There could be nothing so exquisite and so bitter as were my pains. . . . On the other hand, there can be nothing so exquisite and sweet as was my joy" (Alma 36:21).

That joy came about as a result of his contrite repentance. As Elder Hales concluded, "Only by repentance and asking for forgiveness of the Lord was Alma able to put his pain behind him and receive of the joy and light of the gospel. The Lord taught the Nephites that knowledge of the truth, diligent faith, and true repentance bring about a change of heart. Alma experienced a mighty change of heart."[20]

Alma's sobering question is directed to each of us as he asks, "Have you experienced this mighty change in your hearts?" (Alma 5:14). Moving toward that change involves effort on our part. Elder Jack H. Goaslind said,

> Our goodness—our every righteous endeavor—our good works, our obedience, and our efforts to bless others must be anchored in and driven by our faith in Christ, our testimonies of his mission and sacrifice, and our willingness to move off our comfortable plateaus. Until we find ways to strengthen, increase, and magnify our testimonies of Jesus Christ and the effect of the Atonement in our lives, we will be unable to answer Alma's question in the affirmative.[21]

Why is a mighty change of heart so important? Gospel scholars George Reynolds and Janne M. Sjodahl wrote, "The heart is said to be the seat of spiritual light; the source whence springs our love and our devotion, our likes and dislikes, our joy and our sorrows, and our loyalty and fidelity."[22] As the seat of our spiritual light and the source of our devotion and loyalty, it stands to reason that changing the heart is essential if we are to become sanctified and exalted.

As important as it is, such a change is not always easy. In quoting President John Taylor, Elder Neal A. Maxwell said that "the Lord may even choose to wrench our very heartstrings. If our hearts are set too much upon the things

---

20   "Healing Soul and Body."

21   Jack H. Goaslind, "Spiritual Mountaintops," *Ensign*, Nov. 1995, 9.

22   George Reynolds and Janne M. Sjodahl, *Commentary on the Book of Mormon*, arr. by David Sjodahl King (Salt Lake City: Deseret Book, 1973), 3:78.

of this world, they may need to be wrenched, or broken, or undergo a mighty change."[23]

MAKING THE CHANGE ENDURE

After asking his listeners if they had experienced a mighty change of heart, Alma asked a follow-up question that points to the concept of enduring to the end, staying the course, and keeping the commitment: "And now behold, I say unto you, my brethren, if ye have experienced a change of heart, and if ye have felt to sing the song of redeeming love, I would ask, can ye feel so now?" (Alma 5:26).

We are told that disciples must undergo a "mighty change" of heart in order to make for themselves "a new heart" (Ezekiel 18:31; Alma 5:12–14). Once we have done that, why is it not enough to draw on that experience throughout our lives? After all, it's a *mighty* change. And all the words used to define *change*—transform, convert, alter, modify, literally to make something different than it would be if left alone—imply permanence. But we are cautioned,

> [Alma's question] is a call to keep our witness and our experience with the Spirit current and up to date. Though it is important to develop and maintain reservoirs of faith—repositories of memories and experiences and encounters with the divine which have built and strengthened testimony—we must be ever on guard against spiritual lethargy, against coasting upon our memories, against living only in the past. We cannot afford to pause and homestead on spiritual plateaus. Our task is to move on, to progress.[24]

The very process of endurance is critical to our spiritual growth and development. Elder Neal A. Maxwell said,

> On one of those rare occasions when His very voice was heard, the Father testified, "Yea, the words of my Beloved are true and faithful. He that endureth to the end, the same shall be saved" (2 Ne. 31:15.) Of all that the Father might have said, He stressed endurance. Why?
>
> First, because God has repeatedly said He would structure mortality to be a proving and testing experience. . . . He has

23 Neal A. Maxwell, "'Swallowed Up in the Will of the Father'," *Ensign*, Nov. 1995, 22.
24 Joseph F. McConkie and Robert L. Millet, *Doctrinal Commentary on the Book of Mormon* (Salt Lake City: Bookcraft, 1991) 88, 3:32.

carried out His divine intent, hasn't He? Thus, even our fiery trials, said Peter, should not be thought of as "some strange thing" (1 Pet. 4:12). Hence, enduring is vital, and those who so last will be first spiritually!

By taking Jesus' yoke upon us and enduring, we learn most deeply of Him and especially how to be like Him (see Matt. 11:29). Even though our experiences are micro compared to His, the process is the same.[25]

Alma also asked if his listeners had felt to "sing the song of redeeming love" and, if so, "can ye feel so now?" (Alma 5:26). Obviously, one way to "sing the song of redeeming love" is to literally sing the glorious hymns: "Praise ye the Lord: for it is good to sing praises unto our God; for it is pleasant; and praise is comely" (Psalm 147:1). The Lord Himself said, "For my soul delighteth in the song of the heart; yea, the song of the righteous is a prayer unto me, and it shall be answered with a blessing upon their heads. Wherefore, lift up thy heart and rejoice, and cleave unto the covenants which thou hast made" (D&C 25:12–13).

But the phrase as Alma used it means much more. Hugh Nibley taught that *sing the song of redeeming love* is a historical reference to an actual ritual song that existed in ancient Israelite culture:

> It's the old Hebrew *trishagion* (Isaiah quotes this hymn, too, in Isaiah 6:3) as all Israel in the Church unite their voices "and the powers below heaven sing," as the stars join in "this Hymn of the cosmos to God's bounty and love." It's the hymn of redeeming love. See, this is the time of the at-one-ment, when the two worlds come together. . . . They fuse now in glorious music. . . .
>
> We have Alma asking here in Alma 5:26: "If ye have experienced a change of heart, and if ye have felt to sing the song of redeeming love, I would ask, can ye feel so now?" And here we're told in the *Apostolic Constitutions,* "it behooves every man to feel in his heart to send up a song to thee [to feel to sing the song of redeeming love] through Christ for the sake of all; for thou art kind in thy benefactions and generous in thy compassions." And that's the way Alma describes it.[26]

25 Neal A. Maxwell, "Endure It Well," *Ensign*, May 1990.
26 Hugh Nibley, *Teachings of the Book of Mormon, Semester 2 Transcripts* (Provo, Utah: FARMS, 1993), 289–290.

Besides literally singing, what do Saints do when they sing the song of redeeming love? Nephi gave a good example when he said, "And we talk of Christ, we rejoice in Christ, we preach of Christ, we prophesy of Christ, and we write according to our prophecies, that our children may know to what source they may look for a remission of their sins" (2 Nephi 25:26). Nephi went on to say that we should "bow down before him, and worship him with all your might, mind, and strength, and your whole soul; and if ye do this ye shall in nowise be cast out" (2 Nephi 25:28–29).

If we were to sing the song of redeeming love, we would pray with thanksgiving for God the Father loving us so much that He gave us His Son to redeem us from death and hell. We would honor the Savior's Atonement by fully and sincerely repenting. We would echo the words of the Apostle Paul when he said, "For I am not ashamed of the gospel of Christ: for it is the power of God unto salvation to every one that believeth" (Romans 1:16).

We would be faithful disciples of Jesus Christ and follow the counsel He gave John Whitmer through the Prophet Joseph Smith: "And now, behold, I say unto you, that the thing which will be of the most worth unto you will be to declare repentance unto this people, that you may bring souls unto me, that you may rest with them in the kingdom of my Father" (D&C 15:6). We would work to bring souls to Christ on both sides of the veil.

We would follow the counsel of the Lord when He said, "Let thy bowels also be full of charity towards all men, and to the household of faith, and let virtue garnish thy thoughts unceasingly" (D&C 121:45). We would be on the covenant path and would be about doing good.[27] We would enjoy the company of the Holy Spirit as He leads us to do good.[28]

If we experience a mighty change of heart and persist in that change for the rest of our lives, we will enjoy not only the company of the Holy Spirit, but will eventually enjoy the company of the Lord. Enos described being with his beloved Redeemer with these tender words:

> And I soon go to the place of my rest, which is with my Redeemer; for I know that in him I shall rest. And I rejoice in the day when my mortal shall put on immortality, and shall stand before him; then shall I see his face with pleasure, and he will say unto me: Come unto me, ye blessed, there is a place prepared for you in the mansions of my Father. (Enos 1:27)

27 See Alma 7:24.
28 See D&C 11:12.

As we experience a mighty change of heart, we come to regard with importance the things that are important to the Father and His Son. Our hearts yearn for the things for which They yearn. We become one with Them and prepare in every way to be in Their presence. As Elder Neal A. Maxwell said,

> Consider, what if Jesus' Mortal Messiahship had consisted only of remarkable sermons? Or was further enhanced with healings and other miracles—but without Gethsemane's and Calvary's awful but consecrated hours of the Atonement? How then would we regard Jesus' ministry? Where would mankind be?
>
> Brothers and sisters, whatever we embrace instead of Jesus and His work will keep us from qualifying to enter His kingdom and therefore from being embraced by Him. (See Morm. 6:17.)

May we get settled and prepare now for that marvelous moment then.

CHAPTER FOUR
BEING DELIVERED

And now behold, I say unto you, my brethren, you that belong to this church, have you sufficiently retained in remembrance the captivity of your fathers? Yea, and have you sufficiently retained in remembrance his mercy and long-suffering towards them? And moreover, have ye sufficiently retained in remembrance that he has delivered their souls from hell? (Alma 5:6)

ALMA BEGINS HIS SPEECH TO the Nephites at Zarahemla by asking if they remember the hardships their people suffered while in captivity at the hands of the wicked Nephites and the Lamanites. It was an inspired tactic; once he prompted the people to vividly remember that captivity, he was able to teach of the deliverance achieved through the power, goodness, and mercy of God.

Latter-day Saint scholar Louis Midgley underscored the wisdom of Alma's approach, pointing out,

---

ALMA'S QUESTIONS ON CAPTIVITY AND DELIVERANCE

Have you sufficiently retained in remembrance the captivity of your fathers? (See Alma 5:6)

Have you sufficiently retained in remembrance God's mercy and long-suffering toward your fathers? (See Alma 5:6)

Have you sufficiently retained in remembrance that He has delivered their souls from hell? (See Alma 5:6)
Were your fathers destroyed? (See Alma 5:8)

Were the bands of death broken, and the chains of hell which encircled your fathers about, were they loosed? (See Alma 5:9)

"The call to *remember* is often a passionate plea to see God's hand in delivering his people from bondage and captivity."[1]

The theme of captivity is a frequent one in the Book of Mormon; Alma and other Book of Mormon authors mythologized "the captivity of [their] fathers" in Israel.[2] Many of those who contributed to the Book of Mormon—such as Nephi, Abinadi, Limhi, Alma the Elder, Alma the Younger, and Amulek—had endured actual physical bondage themselves.

It's important to recognize that not all bondage—defined by Webster as "the state of being bound by or subjected to some external power or control"— is physical. Bondage imagery is found in Alma 5 and abounds in the Book of Mormon, illustrating the many different forms of bondage: "the bands of death,"[3] "the bonds of iniquity,"[4] "the chains of hell,"[5] the "snares" of the devil,[6] and satanic "captivity."[7] In the spirit world, the wicked are confined to "prison."[8] And, of course, there is the physical bondage represented by the slavery or involuntary servitude that the earlier Nephites had suffered.

Alma wanted the Nephites he was addressing to understand the concept of being delivered, and to do so he had to prompt them to remember the captivity of their forefathers. Remembering was essential because, as Midgley pointed out, Alma's audience was not personally acquainted with captivity:

> Because these Nephites of Alma's time were distant from
> God's acts of deliverance in the past and from the redemption
> promised in the future to their descendants, they had to rely
> on the words of prophets, the visions of seers, and what was
> recorded in the sacred texts. So formal remembrance took
> on crucial significance for them. Acts of remembering could
> let them feel as if they were participating in the past events
> that saved their forefathers. Meanwhile, remembering the
> prophecies could help them look forward to the events that
> had not yet taken place. Through remembering the bondage

---

1   Louis C. Midgley, "The Ways of Remembrance," in *Rediscovering the Book of Mormon*, eds. John L. Sorenson and Melvin J. Thorne (Salt Lake City: Deseret Book and FARMS, 1991), 169.

2   See Mosiah 27:16; Alma 5:5–9; 29:11–13; 36:28–30.

3   Alma 5:7, 9, 10. See also Mosiah 15:8; 16:7; Alma 7:12; 11:41–42; Mormon 9:13.

4   See Mosiah 23:13; 27:29; Alma 36:27; 41:11; Mormon 8:31; Moroni 8:14; see also Acts 8:23.

5   Alma 5:7. See also 2 Nephi 1:13; 9:25; 28:19, 22; Alma 12:6, 11, 17; 13:30; 36:18; see also D&C 123:8.

6   See Alma 10:17; 12:6; Helaman 3:29; see also 2 Timothy 2:26.

7   See 1 Nephi 13:5; 2 Nephi 2:27–29; 9:12; Alma 12:11; 3 Nephi 18:15; 27:32; see also John 8:34; Romans 7:23; Moses 4:4.

8   See Isaiah 24:22; 49:9; 61:1; 1 Peter 3:19; Alma 40:13–14.

and captivity and then deliverance of their fathers—from Egypt and from Jerusalem as well as from the desert wilderness and ocean—the Nephites would have their minds turned ahead to the atoning sacrifice of Jesus Christ—the central event in the overall plan of redeeming men from bondage to sin and death.[9]

WE MUST REMEMBER THAT IT IS THE LORD WHO DELIVERS

Immediately after introducing himself to his audience, in Alma 5:4–5 Alma talked about his father's remarkable experience helping the Nephites escape captivity to King Noah. As a young boy, Alma must have been deeply impressed by this amazing story of deliverance of his family. It's a richly detailed account we would also do well to remember.

> Now Alma, having been warned of the Lord that the armies of king Noah would come upon them, and having made it known to his people, therefore they gathered together their flocks, and took of their grain, and departed into the wilderness before the armies of king Noah.
>
> And the Lord did strengthen them, that the people of king Noah could not overtake them to destroy them.
>
> And they fled eight days' journey into the wilderness. (Mosiah 23:1–3)

Note that in this case of deliverance, the Lord did not destroy or divert the armies of King Noah. Instead, he strengthened Alma and his people so that they could effectively escape the pursuing army. The Lord's actions in this case illustrate that His deliverance manifests in different ways.

Once established at their destination, the Nephites prospered in the land they called Helam, and they built a mighty city, which they also called Helam. When the people pleaded with Alma the Elder to become their king, he refused, reminding them of the captivity they had so recently escaped:

> And now I say unto you, ye have been oppressed by king Noah, and have been in bondage to him and his priests, and have been brought into iniquity by them; therefore ye were bound with the bands of iniquity.

9   Louis C. Midgley, "The Ways of Remembrance," in *Rediscovering the Book of Mormon*, eds. John L. Sorenson and Melvin J. Thorne (Salt Lake City: Deseret Book and FARMS, 1991), 169–170.

> And now as ye have been delivered by the power of God
> out of these bonds; yea, even out of the hands of king Noah
> and his people, and also from the bonds of iniquity, even so
> I desire that ye should stand fast in this liberty wherewith ye
> have been made free, and that ye trust no man to be a king
> over you. (Mosiah 23:12–13)

The people continued to prosper until, while tilling their land, they saw a Lamanite army at the border of their land. Fleeing from their fields in fear, they gathered in the city of Helam.[10] Alma the Elder stood in the middle of them "and exhorted them that they should not be frightened, but that they should remember the Lord their God and he would deliver them" (Mosiah 23:27). Comforted by Alma's words, "they hushed their fears, and began to cry unto the Lord that he would soften the hearts of the Lamanites, that they would spare them, and their wives, and their children" (Mosiah 23:28).

When Alma and his people surrendered to the army, the hearts of the Lamanites were softened. Though the Lamanites used their military prowess to take over the land of Helam, the Nephites lived on the land in peace—until the Lamanites "began to increase in riches, and began to trade one with another and wax great, and began to be a cunning and a wise people . . . delighting in all manner of wickedness and plunder" (Mosiah 24:7).

Buoyed with confidence because of their various successes, the Lamanite leader at that time, Amulon, started to exercise authority over and persecute Alma and his people, putting punishing tasks on them and appointing brutal taskmasters over them. The afflictions of the Nephites became so great that they "began to cry mightily to God" (Mosiah 24:10). When he and his men saw the people praying, Amulon demanded that they stop their praying, and he put guards over them to make sure they obeyed his edict. He instructed that "whosoever should be found calling upon God should be put to death" (Mosiah 24:11).

Instead of vocalizing their prayers, the people of Alma poured out their hearts to God—who, of course, knew the thoughts of their hearts. What followed is one of the most stunning examples of delivery in all of scripture, demonstrating that "deliverance" takes many forms and can come before the actual freedom from bondage:

> And it came to pass that the voice of the Lord came to them
> in their afflictions, saying: Lift up your heads and be of good

---

10   See Mosiah 23:24–26.

comfort, for I know of the covenant which ye have made unto me; and I will covenant with my people and deliver them out of bondage.

And I will also ease the burdens which are put upon your shoulders, that even you cannot feel them upon your backs, even while you are in bondage; and this will I do that ye may stand as witnesses for me hereafter, and that ye may know of a surety that I, the Lord God, do visit my people in their afflictions.

And now it came to pass that the burdens which were laid upon Alma and his brethren were made light; yea, the Lord did strengthen them that they could bear up their burdens with ease, and they did submit cheerfully and with patience to all the will of the Lord.

And it came to pass that so great was their faith and their patience that the voice of the Lord came unto them again, saying: Be of good comfort, for on the morrow I will deliver you out of bondage.

And he said unto Alma: Thou shalt go before this people, and I will go with thee and deliver this people out of bondage.

Now it came to pass that Alma and his people in the night-time gathered their flocks together, and also of their grain; yea, even all the night-time were they gathering their flocks together.

And in the morning the Lord caused a deep sleep to come upon the Lamanites, yea, and all their task-masters were in a profound sleep.

And Alma and his people departed into the wilderness; and when they had traveled all day they pitched their tents in a valley, and they called the valley Alma, because he led their way in the wilderness.

Yea, and in the valley of Alma they poured out their thanks to God because he had been merciful unto them, and eased their burdens, and had delivered them out of bondage; for they were in bondage, and none could deliver them except it were the Lord their God. (Mosiah 24:13–21)

This incident also shows the variety of ways in which the Lord delivers. Even before He helped the people escape the Lamanites, the Lord eased their burdens, making them light. He also strengthened the people that they could bear the burdens. Once again, it was the Lord who engineered the deliverance—this time an actual escape—by causing a deep sleep to come upon the Lamanites so the Nephites could get away undetected.

While Alma did not rehearse all the details of that deliverance as we have them in the scriptures to his audience in Zarahemla, he did say that his father's people "were delivered out of the hands of the people of king Noah, by the mercy and power of God" (Alma 5:4). Then he posed this question:

> And now behold, I say unto you, my brethren, you that belong to this church, have you sufficiently retained in remembrance the captivity of your fathers? Yea, and have you sufficiently retained in remembrance his mercy and long-suffering towards them? And moreover, have ye sufficiently retained in remembrance that he has delivered their souls from hell? (Alma 5:6)

This question surely was ringing in the ears of Moroni five centuries later when he exhorted us, "Behold, I would exhort you that when ye shall read these things, if it be wisdom in God that ye should read them, that ye would remember how merciful the Lord hath been unto the children of men" (Moroni 10:3).

Why is remembering so important in helping us live the gospel of Jesus Christ? President Spencer W. Kimball stated, "When you look in the dictionary for the most important word, do you know what it is? . . . 'Remember' is the word."[11] Remembering brings inspiration and gratitude into our souls and helps us stay on the straight and narrow path, which is the covenant path.

It's also essential that we remember, else we will find ourselves mired in the quicksand of sin. Remembering where our strength is and from whom it comes helps us understand how the devil works and how to withstand his strategies. The words of Helaman (Alma's grandson) to his sons Lehi and Nephi (Alma's great-grandsons) speak volumes:

> And now, my sons, *remember, remember* that it is upon the rock of our Redeemer, who is Christ, the Son of God, that ye must build your foundation; that when the devil shall send forth his mighty winds, yea, his shafts in the whirlwind, yea, when all his hail and his mighty storm shall beat upon you, it shall have no power over you to drag you down to the gulf

---

11   Spencer W. Kimball, "Circles of Exaltation," [Brigham Young University address to religious educators, Jun. 28, 1968], 8.

of misery and endless wo, because of the rock upon which ye
are built, which is a sure foundation, a foundation whereon if
men build they cannot fall. (Helaman 5:12; emphasis added)

Several ordinances, covenants, and commandments work together to assist
us in remembering God the Father and Christ the Lord. One purpose of the
ordinance of the sacrament is to help us remember the Savior's sacrifice. President
David O. McKay called the sacrament "one of the most sacred ordinances of
the Church" and said, "Too few communicants attach to this simple though
sublime rite the importance and significance that it merits. Unfortunately, the
form of worship is frequently an outward compliance without the true soul
acknowledgment of its deep spiritual significance."[12]

Praying also helps us remember the goodness of God, as does studying the
scriptures, which is why we should feast upon them every day[13] and live by
every word of the instruction we find there.[14] Being single-minded also helps us
remember as our whole bodies are filled with light.[15] The temple and the sacred
covenants we make there also assist us in remembering, as does the garment,
which reminds us of the sacred covenants made in the temple and helps protect
us from temptation.

WHAT BEING DELIVERED LOOKS LIKE

Referring to his father's people, who were delivered from captivity, Alma
shared with his listeners how that deliverance was accomplished, in a verse that
is packed with rich meaning and imagery. Speaking of how the Lord delivered
the people, Alma said,

> Behold, he changed their hearts; yea, he awakened them out of
> a deep sleep, and they awoke unto God. Behold, they were in
> the midst of darkness; nevertheless, their souls were illuminated
> by the light of the everlasting word; yea, they were encircled
> about by the bands of death, and the chains of hell, and an
> everlasting destruction did await them. (Alma 5:7)

In describing the deliverance, Alma first clarified that the Lord "changed
their hearts." That is possible for the Lord, of course, because the Lord "seeth
not as man seeth; for man looketh on the outward appearance, but the Lord

---

12   David O. McKay, "Gospel Ideals," *Improvement Era,* 71.
13   See 2 Nephi 32:3.
14   See D&C 84:43–46.
15   D&C 88:67–68.

looketh on the heart" (1 Samuel 16:7). The Lord is interested in our intents and desires much more than our deeds and actions. This concept was at the center of Christ's mortal ministry—it was no longer sufficient to dutifully abide by the letter of the law;[16] instead, Christ's temple worthiness demanded not only "clean hands" but also "a pure heart" (Psalm 24:4; 2 Nephi 25:16).

In changing the hearts of these people, the Lord "awakened them out of a deep sleep, and they awoke unto God." Hebrew writers often used the word *sleep* figuratively to denote "death" or "moral slackness, indolence, or stupid inactivity of the wicked."[17] Thus, Book of Mormon prophets often used the word *awake*—the opposite of *sleep*—in the call to repent and renew covenants.[18] In his oft-quoted metaphor of likening the word of God to a seed, Alma used a similar phrase: "If ye will *awake* and *arouse your faculties,* even to an experiment upon my words" (Alma 32:27; emphasis added). Just as a seed germinates, sprouts, and begins to grow, our spirits emerge out of darkness, unawareness, and inactivity when we wake up and become spiritually alive. The process of awaking is often the beginning of making the mighty change. It is part of the desire to become like Christ. It was demonstrated by King Benjamin's people when they were awakened by his words to the point that they had no desire to sin but to do good continually.[19]

In addressing his audience, Alma used another interesting phrase: "their souls were illuminated by the light of the everlasting word" (Alma 5:7). The association of *the word* with *light* is an ancient one: "Thy word is a lamp unto my feet, and a light unto my path" (Psalm 119:105). The power of the word of God to illuminate the way we should live our lives makes the light metaphor an obvious one. A passage in the Doctrine and Covenants contains a couplet that highlights this association: "The word of the Lord is truth, and whatsoever is truth is light" (D&C 84:45). Carried to its conclusion, we come to a greater understanding: if *the word* is *truth* and *truth* is *light*, then the word is *light*.

Alma seems to be particularly fond of the word-light association. In his sermon to the Zoramites, Alma taught that one of the identifying characteristics of the word of God is its capacity to "enlighten [one's] understanding" (Alma 32:28). Alma also teaches that by tasting the "delicious"

---

16   See Matthew 5:21–48.

17   Merrill F. Unger, *The New Unger's Bible Dictionary*, rev. ed., R. K. Harrison, ed. (Chicago: Moody Bible Institute of Chicago, 1957), 1032.

18   See 2 Nephi 4:28; 9:47; Jacob 3:11; Mosiah 2:38, 40; 4:5; Alma 4:3; 7:22; 32:27; Ether 8:24; Moroni 10:31.

19   See Mosiah 5:2.

fruit of the seed, one could be assured of its goodness.[20] Later in that sermon, he equates tasting the seed, or the "word," with "tasting light."[21] As Alma relates it, when the people received the word of God through Abinadi, Alma the Elder and his followers proved its goodness, for "their souls were illuminated by the light of the everlasting word" (Alma 5:7). Alma's theory of the word's illuminating power in Alma 32 seems deduced from his father's experience with the word as recounted in Alma 5.

Alma described his father's people in captivity as "encircled about by the bands of death, and the chains of hell" (Alma 5:7). Notice that he does not use the word *yoke* but instead uses "bands" and "chains," which words seem to describe actual enslavement. In their collective and shared histories, Alma's listeners had enough experience with redemption, bondage and deliverance, and captivity and freedom that they could understand the importance of what he was saying.

Both Nephi and Jacob used the phrase *chains of hell*,[22] but Alma repeatedly used it in his doctrinal discourses, particularly in Alma 12.[23] Alma even defined the term in his sermon to the people of Ammonihah when he said that those who harden their hearts are "given the lesser portion of the word until they know nothing concerning his mysteries; and then they are taken captive by the devil, and led by his will down to destruction. Now this is what is meant by the chains of hell" (Alma 12:11). To be "encircled about by . . . the chains of hell," then, is to be easily deceived by the devil because of our own ignorance regarding spiritual

ALMA'S QUESTIONS ON FAITH

And was he [Abinadi] not a holy prophet? (See Alma 5:11)

Did he not speak the words of God? (See Alma 5:11)

Did not my father Alma believe in the words of Abinadi when he spoke the words of God? (See Alma 5:11)

What grounds had they to hope for salvation? (See Alma 5:10)

Do you exercise faith in the redemption of Him who created you? (See Alma 5:15)

Do you look forward with an eye of faith? (See Alma 5:15)

---

20   See Alma 32:28.

21   See Alma 32:28; 33:22–23. See John W. Welch and J. Gregory Welch, *Charting in the Book of Mormon* (Provo, Utah: FARMS, 1999), chart 52; see also Alma 32:35

22   See 2 Nephi 1:13; 9:45; 28:19.

23   See Alma 12:6, 11, 17; see also Alma 13:30; 36:18.

matters. The only way we can be freed from that bondage is through the redeeming and saving power of Christ.

Of the type of change Alma described, in which the Lord delivers people, C. S. Lewis wrote that as we mature in spiritual things and begin to transform into new creatures through Christ,

> we begin to notice, besides our particular sinful acts, our sinfulness; begin to be alarmed not only about what we do, but about what we are. . . . And if (as I said before) what we are matters even more than what we do—if, indeed, what we do matters chiefly as evidence of what we are—then it follows that the change which I most need to undergo is a change that my own direct, voluntary efforts cannot bring about. . . . I cannot, by direct, moral effort, give myself new motives. After the first few steps in the Christian life, we realize that everything which really needs to be done in our souls can be done only by God.[24]

WE ARE DELIVERED BY EXERCISING FAITH TO THE END

After describing death and captivity and the power of God to deliver, Alma tells his listeners, then and now, that it is our own faith that serves as a catalyst to deliverance. He asks his listeners a series of questions designed to move their attention from faith in the living prophet (in their case, Abinadi) to the overall principle of faith—and, specifically, faith in the Atonement of Jesus Christ.[25]

Along with the Apostle Paul, Alma the Younger is perhaps the best-known exponent of the principle of faith among all of God's chosen prophets. His stirring discourse on this subject before the ostracized Zoramites continues to this day to resonate with power among the honest-in-heart: "And now as I said concerning faith—faith is not to have a perfect knowledge of things; therefore if ye have faith ye hope for things which are not seen, which are true" (Alma 32:21).

Alma then proceeds to unfold to the people a remarkable analogy between faith and the planting and cultivating of a seed—which sprouts and evolves, through faithful devotion, until it becomes "a tree springing up unto everlasting life" (Alma 32:41). In connection with faith, Alma, as high priest of the Church, gives definitive teachings on a variety of subjects, including the transforming power

---

24   C. S. Lewis, *Mere Christianity* (New York: HarperCollins Publishers, 1952), 164–165.
25   See Alma 5:11–12, 15.

of spiritual conversion, the atoning sacrifice of the Redeemer, foreordination of the righteous, the "virtue of the word of God" (Alma 31:5) to effect miraculous change, the sure pathway to happiness, and life after death. In all he teaches, Alma connects all good works and righteousness to faith.

Another example of astonishing faith is the Prophet Abinadi. Around 150 BC, the Lord sent Abinadi to the land of Nephi to preach repentance and warn the people against the inevitable destructive outcomes of their behavior. Abinadi's compelling words were rejected, he was accused, and he fled for his own safety. Two years later, however, he returned in disguise, enabling him to reenter the city of Nephi long enough to convey the dire pronouncement of the Lord: "And it shall come to pass that except they repent I will utterly destroy them from off the face of the earth" (Mosiah 12:8).

On that second occasion, Abinadi was fearless, and he converted one of Noah's priests, Alma, who at that time was a young man. Later that Alma would become the father of Alma the Younger, the great Nephite prophet, priest, and leader. As Abinadi was being put to death, he told King Noah and his priests, "Yea, and I will suffer even until death, and I will not recall my words, and they shall stand as a testimony against you. And if ye slay me ye will shed innocent blood, and this shall also stand as a testimony against you at the last day" (Mosiah 17:10). We know the result: he was burned at the stake, a martyr for the cause of truth. Before he expired, he prophesied, "Behold, even as ye have done unto me, so shall it come to pass that thy seed shall cause that many shall suffer the pains that I do suffer, even the pains of death by fire; and this because they believe in the salvation of the Lord their God" (Mosiah 17:15).

Abinadi's words were fulfilled when King Noah was burned to death by his own rebellious subjects[26] and when the armies of the Lamanites killed many of the warriors from the city of Nephi.[27]

His experience and the fulfillment of his words leave no doubt that Abinadi was a prophet and spoke the words of God.

Alma then asks rhetorically whether his father believed the words of Abinadi. We know the answer, for it is given in scripture: "But there was one among them whose name was Alma, . . . and he believed the words which Abinadi had spoken" (Mosiah 17:2).

He believed. Faith in the Lord is where it always begins. Faith is the first great principle of the gospel of Jesus Christ. Faith leads us to repentance.[28] Faith

---

26   See Mosiah 19:20.

27   See Mosiah 21:7–12.

28   See Alma 34:15–17.

is the beginning of change. Our Heavenly Father and our Savior work with us according to our faith.[29] As we fast and pray, we become firm in our faith,[30] and when we hear and feast upon the word of God, our faith increases.[31]

Our hearkening to the words of prophets demonstrates our faith in the Lord. Christ Himself said, "For he that receiveth my servants receiveth me" (D&C 84:36). The Lord commends those who believe in His servants when He says, "blessed are they who shall believe in your words, and come down into the depths of humility and be baptized, for they shall be visited with fire and with the Holy Ghost, and shall receive a remission of their sins" (3 Nephi 12:2). The Lord also reminds us, "whether by mine own voice or by the voice of my servants, it is the same" (D&C 1:38).

As Alma continues introducing his discourse, he repeats twice the point that his father believed the words of the Prophet Abinadi: "Did not my father Alma believe in the words which were delivered by the mouth of Abinadi? . . . Did he not speak the words of God, and my father Alma believe them?" (Alma 5:11). Alma wanted to make sure the people of Zarahemla knew that his father believed the words of the Prophet Abinadi.[32] Later in his speech, Alma helps his listeners know how to receive truth by reiterating how he himself received a testimony of the truth of all things by the power of the Holy Ghost:

> Behold, I say unto you they are made known unto me by the Holy Spirit of God. Behold, I have fasted and prayed many days that I might know these things of myself. And now I do know of myself that they are true; for the Lord God hath made them manifest unto me by his Holy Spirit; and this is the spirit of revelation which is in me.
>
> And moreover, I say unto you that it has thus been revealed unto me, that the words which have been spoken by our fathers are true, even so according to the spirit of prophecy which is in me, which is also by the manifestation of the Spirit of God. (Alma 5:46–47)

Alma, along with other Book of Mormon prophets, understood Christ's dual role as Creator and Redeemer. With that understanding, he asks his listeners, "Do ye exercise faith in the redemption of him who created you?

---

29   See Ether 12:29.
30   See Helaman 3:35.
31   See Romans 10:17.
32   See Mosiah 17:2.

Do you look forward with an eye of faith, and view this mortal body raised in immortality, and this corruption raised in incorruption, to stand before God to be judged according to the deeds which have been done in the mortal body?" (Alma 5:15).

At the outset of the Book of Mormon, Nephi establishes a holistic attitude among his people that balanced strict adherence to the law of Moses and faithful anticipation of Christ's coming. He explains, "And, notwithstanding we believe in Christ, we keep the law of Moses, and look forward with steadfastness unto Christ, until the law shall be fulfilled" (2 Nephi 25:24). In this scheme, the true function of the law of Moses was fulfilled—that of "pointing [their] souls to [Christ]" (Jacob 4:5; see also Jarom 1:11). This attitude continued among righteous Book of Mormon peoples like the Ammonites, who likewise "did keep the law of Moses . . . for it was not yet all fulfilled. But notwithstanding the law of Moses, they did look forward to the coming of Christ" (Alma 25:15).

Looking forward to Christ and His power to redeem both body and spirit thus became a defining characteristic of those faithful to Nephi's righteous tradition. The prophets Jarom and Benjamin put an interesting spin on this concept: "look forward unto the Messiah, and believe in him to come *as though he already was*" (Jarom 1:11; emphasis added), and "whosoever should believe that Christ should come, *the same might receive remission of their sins . . . even as though he had already come among them*" (Mosiah 3:13; emphasis added).

In Alma's speech, he challenges his audience to "look forward with an eye of faith" (Alma 5:15). Alma's statement challenged their faith to an even greater degree, asking them to look even beyond Christ's mortal advent to the day of His immortal advent—the day of resurrection and judgment and eternal reward.

The phrase *eye of faith* appears only two other times in all of scripture—in Alma's sermon to the Zoramite poor[33] and in Moroni's abridgment of the book of Ether.[34] In the Bible, *eye* is sometimes used in connection with the heart or mind.[35] The "eye of faith," then, describes a heart full of faith. It is the eyes of light and hope, with a consecrated focus on serving the Lord as our single Master, that we lay up treasures in His glorious heaven.[36]

Elder Neal A. Maxwell used the same phrase in his testimony of the Savior when he said, "Granted, those with true hope still see their personal circumstances shaken at times—like a kaleidoscope. Yet with the 'eye of faith,' even in their changed, proximate circumstances, they still see divine design."[37]

---

33 See Alma 32:40.

34 See Ether 12:19.

35 See Ecclesiastes 1:8; Luke 19:42; Ephesians 1:18. See also "Eye" in *The HarperCollins Bible Dictionary*, 320.

36 See 3 Nephi 12:19–24.

37 Neal A. Maxwell, "Hope through the Atonement of Jesus Christ," *Ensign*, Nov. 1998, 61.

The Lord commanded that all men "must repent, and be baptized in his name, having perfect faith in the Holy One of Israel, or they cannot be saved in the kingdom of God" (2 Nephi 9:23). The Prophet Joseph Smith discussed three degrees of faith in teaching how to exercise that kind of faith. Regarding the first degree, or facet, of faith, the Prophet said,

> Let us here offer some explanation in relation to faith, that our meaning may be clearly comprehended. We ask, then, what are we to understand by a man's working by faith? We answer—*we understand that when a man works by faith he works by mental exertion instead of physical force. It is by words, instead of exerting his physical powers,* with which every being works when he works by faith. God said, "Let there be light, and there was light." Joshua spake, and the "great lights which God had created stood still. Elijah commanded, and the heavens were stayed for the space of three years and six months, so that it did not rain: he again commanded and the heavens gave forth rain. All this was done by faith." . . . Faith, then, works by words; and with these its mightiest works have been, and will be, performed.[38]

Of the second degree of faith, the Prophet Joseph said, "Faith is the moving cause of all action . . . in intelligent beings."[39] James surely understood that faith and works are inseparably connected when he stated,

> Even so faith, if it hath not works, is dead, being alone.
>
> Yea, a man may say, Thou hast faith, and I have works: shew me thy faith without thy works, and I will shew thee my faith by my works.
>
> Thou believest that there is one God; thou doest well: the devils also believe, and tremble.
>
> But wilt thou know, O vain man, that faith without works is dead?
>
> Was not Abraham our father justified by works, when he had offered Isaac his son upon the altar?
>
> Seest thou how faith wrought with his works, and by works was faith made perfect?
>
> And the scripture was fulfilled which saith, Abraham believed God, and it was imputed unto him for righteousness: and he was called the Friend of God.

---

38   *Lectures on Faith* [1985], 7:3; emphasis added.
39   *Lectures on Faith*, 1:8.

Ye see then how that by works a man is justified, and not by faith only.

Likewise also was not Rahab the harlot justified by works, when she had received the messengers, and had sent *them* out another way?

For as the body without the spirit is dead, so faith without works is dead also. (James 2:17–26)

The third degree of faith is the principle and source of power.[40] The Prophet Joseph Smith said,

Faith, then, is the first great governing principle which has power, dominion, and authority over all things: by it they exist, by it they are upheld, by it they are changed, or by it they remain, agreeably to the will of God. Without it, there is no power, and without power there could be no creation, nor existence.[41]

From this statement we learn that all things are governed by faith and are subsequently governed by God. Faith is the governing principle of power. Thus, we need to understand that God works with His children according to our faith.[42]

Faith is fully utilized when all three degrees are applied. The Prophet Joseph went on to teach that "Faith, then, is the first great governing principle which has power, dominion, and authority over all things; by it they exist, by it they are upheld, by it they are changed or by it they remain agreeable to the will of God."[43]

Faith is a principle of virtue and power, which is why the early Apostles pleaded with the Lord to increase their faith.[44] Faith is so important that the Lord works with all of mankind according to their faith. It is for this reason that our modern prophets equally emphasize the importance of increasing our faith in the Lord Jesus Christ. On October 6, 2018, President Russell M. Nelson posted on social media, "The long-standing objective of the Church is to assist all members to increase their faith in our Lord Jesus Christ and in

---

40   See *Lectures on Faith*, 1:15.
41   *Lectures on Faith*, 1:24.
42   See Enos 1:18; Jarom 1:4; Mosiah 27:14; Alma 12:30; 14:28; 57:21; 3 Nephi 5:14; Mormon 9:37; Ether 12:29.
43   *Lectures on Faith*, 1:24.
44   See Luke 17:5.

His Atonement, to assist them in making and keeping their covenants with God, and to strengthen and seal their families."[45]

WE ARE DELIVERED THROUGH THE ATONEMENT OF JESUS CHRIST

After describing the deliverance of his father's people, Alma asks his listeners,

> And now I ask of you, my brethren, were they destroyed? Behold, I say unto you, Nay, they were not.
>
> And again I ask, were the bands of death broken, and the chains of hell which encircled them about, were they loosed? I say unto you, Yea, they were loosed, and their souls did expand, and they did sing redeeming love. And I say unto you that they are saved. (Alma 5:8–9)

They were saved. They were freed from death and hell. Their sins were wiped clean through the blood of the Lamb[46] and the Atonement of the Lord, for He is mighty to save.[47]

Jacob explains what would have happened if there had been no Atonement of the Lord Jesus Christ when he said,

> Wherefore, it must needs be an infinite atonement—save it should be an infinite atonement this corruption could not put on incorruption. Wherefore, the first judgment which came upon man must needs have remained to an endless duration. And if so, this flesh must have laid down to rot and to crumble to its mother earth, to rise no more.
>
> O the wisdom of God, his mercy and grace! For behold, if the flesh should rise no more our spirits must become subject to that angel who fell from before the presence of the Eternal God, and became the devil, to rise no more.
>
> And our spirits must have become like unto him, and we become devils, angels to a devil, to be shut out from the presence of our God, and to remain with the father of lies, in misery, like unto himself; yea, to that being who beguiled our first parents, who transformeth himself nigh unto an angel of light, and stirreth up the children of men unto secret combinations of murder and all manner of secret works of darkness.

45   Russell M. Nelson, "Opening Remarks," *Ensign* or *Liahona*, Nov. 2018.
46   See Alma 34:6; Ether 13:10–11.
47   See 2 Nephi 31:19.

O how great the goodness of our God, who prepareth a way for our escape from the grasp of this awful monster; yea, that monster, death and hell, which I call the death of the body, and also the death of the spirit." (2 Nephi 9:7–10)

The only way to receive the grace of God that is extended through the Savior's Atonement is by exercising faith unto repentance. Repentance (which is facilitated by the grace of God) and the Lord's grace are both important factors as we remain faithful to the end. Note that the common ingredient is the grace that is offered through the Atonement.

As Alma addresses his audience, he tells them that his father "preached the word unto your fathers, and a mighty change was also wrought in their hearts, and they humbled themselves and put their trust in the true and living God. And behold, they were faithful until the end; therefore they were saved" (Alma 5:13).

What roles do our faith and endurance play? We are told that we are saved through the grace of God after all we can do.[48] *All we can do* requires us to have faith unto repentance with a broken heart and contrite spirit;[49] it requires that we witness to the Father that we are willing to take the name of Christ upon us and receive the Holy Ghost[50] and to do all that is within our power to love God and to do the will of our Heavenly Father. Through this process we are born again,[51] and if we continue to serve the Lord to the end of our mortal lives,[52] we will enjoy a lifetime of faithful discipleship and everlasting salvation and eternal life in the world to come.[53]

Without the grace of God, *all we can do* would consist only of empty or inadequate offerings. Addressing his sons shortly before his death, Lehi emphasizes the great importance of making

these things known unto the inhabitants of the earth, that they may know that there is no flesh that can dwell in the presence of God, save it be through the merits, and mercy, and grace of the Holy Messiah, who layeth down his life according to the flesh, and taketh it again by the power of the Spirit, that he may bring

48 See 2 Nephi 25:23. See Brent J. Schmidt, *Relational Grace: The Reciprocal and Binding Covenant of Charis* (Provo, Utah: BYU Studies, 2017).
49 See Alma 34:15–17; D&C 20:37.
50 See 2 Nephi 31:13.
51 See Mosiah 5:7; 27:25.
52 See D&C 20:37; Mosiah 4:6.
53 See Mosiah 5:15.

to pass the resurrection of the dead, being the first that should rise. (2 Nephi 2:8)[54]

In Alma 5, Alma similarly asks on what grounds we are able to hope for salvation.[55] There is only one answer: we have hope through Christ the Lord.[56] "When we build our lives upon our Savior Jesus Christ, we have hope—a perfect brightness of hope which fills us with light. Hope is an attitude that can create a power and motivation to go forward and endure.[57] . . . to have the power to cope with adversity, our lives must be riveted to hope, which is an anchor for our souls. Hope is not a platitude of simply having a positive attitude; rather, it is rooted in Christ."[58] We are to seek hope through Christ's Atonement.

In a devotional address at Brigham Young University, Elder Neal A. Maxwell spoke of the arduous, unfinished journey all of us face as we go throughout mortality. "The trek awaits," he said, "whether one is rich or poor, short or tall, thin or fat, black or white or brown, old or young, shy or bold, married or single, a prodigal or an ever faithful." Compared to this journey, he said, "all other treks are but a brief walk in a mortal park or are merely time on a telestial treadmill."[59]

The hallmark of that journey, what makes it possible for all of us to complete it in a way that allows us to move on to exaltation, is the Savior's "infinite Atonement" (2 Nephi 9:7; 25:16; Alma 34:12). In the endless end, it is what gives us eternal hope. As Elder Maxwell so eloquently concluded,

> Oh, how we adore Jesus for his atonement! For his free gift of immortality to all! Consider for a moment, how would we regard Christ without the reality of his atonement and resurrection? How would we regard the Sermon on the Mount without the resurrection of the sermon giver *and* eventually all of us? Without the reality of God's plan of salvation and Jesus' atonement, how could the meek truly inherit the earth? How could the pure in heart really see God?[60]

54   See also 2 Nephi 31:19; Moroni 6:4.
55   See Alma 5:10.
56   See Jeremiah 17:7; 1 Timothy 1:1; Titus 1:2; 1 Peter 1:3; 2 Nephi 31:20; Jacob 2:19; Moroni 7:3, 44, 48.
57   See 2 Nephi 31:20.
58   Membermissionaries.org.resources/living-word-table-contents/living-word-chapter-8.
59   Neal A. Maxwell, "In Him All Things Hold Together," [Brigham Young University devotional, March 31, 1991],1, speeches.byu.edu.
60   Neal A. Maxwell, "In Him All Things Hold Together," 1.

CHAPTER FIVE

DECIDING TO WHOSE FLOCK WE BELONG

Behold, I say unto you, that the good shepherd doth call you; yea, and in his own name he doth call you, which is the name of Christ; and if ye will not hearken unto the voice of the good shepherd, to the name by which ye are called, behold, ye are not the sheep of the good shepherd. (Alma 5:38)

EVEN IF WE DON'T REALIZE it, each of us belongs to a flock, and each of us follows the shepherd of that flock. As Alma made abundantly clear to the Nephites in Zarahemla, if they did not hearken to the voice of the Good Shepherd, they were not His sheep. Simply, they were not of His flock. And since Alma taught that there are ultimately only two flocks, it stands to reason that there are only two shepherds. The doctrine of the Two Ways, which can be found repeatedly throughout the Book of Mormon, constantly invites all people to choose to belong to the flock of the Good Shepherd.

And "belonging" should not be understood as something static or automatic. A person must long to belong. A group must work to cohere together. Webster defines a *flock* as "a group of animals of one kind, especially sheep or birds." Being "determined

> ## ALMA'S QUESTIONS ON THE FLOCK AND THE SHEPHERD
>
> If you are not the sheep of the good shepherd, of what fold are you? (See Alma 5:39)
>
> The devil is your shepherd, and you are of his fold; and now who can deny this? (See Alma 5:39)
>
> What shepherd is there having many sheep doth not watch over them, that the wolves enter not and devour his flock? (See Alma 5:59)
>
> If a wolf enter his flock doth the shepherd not drive him out? (See Alma 5:59)

in one mind and in one heart, united in all things" (2 Nephi 1:21) brings the followers of Christ into a unity of the faith. The word *flock* is also defined as a large number of people, especially a body of Christians regarded as the pastoral charge of a religious leader, and used as a verb, it means "to gather together or move in a flock." We, as sheep, must listen to the Shepherd's call, heed His warnings, and follow His guidance, if we expect to remain in His flock and not wander astray into strange places.

THE CONDITION OF SHEEP WITHOUT A SHEPHERD

Alma obviously knew the importance of a shepherd; he told his listeners, "O ye workers of iniquity; ye that are puffed up in the vain things of the world, ye that have professed to have known the ways of righteousness nevertheless have gone astray, as sheep having no shepherd" (Alma 5:37). Without a shepherd, sheep are vulnerable and soon perish.

Alma wasn't the first or only person in holy writ to paint the image of sheep in the lost and desperate state of being without a shepherd. Moses wrote of the importance of having a leader over a congregation "which may go in before them, and which may lead them out, and which may bring them in; that the congregation of the Lord be not as *sheep which have no shepherd*" (Numbers 27:16–17; emphasis added).[1]

Sheep who wander without the direction of a shepherd will become lost, just as covenant people without divine counsel will be lost.[2] To survive, sheep need each other individually, just as they need a wise shepherd collectively. Limhi aptly used the image of sheep without a shepherd to describe "how blind and impenetrable are the understandings of the children of men; for they will not seek wisdom, neither do they desire that she should rule over them! Yea, *they are as a wild flock which fleeth from the shepherd*, and scattereth, and are driven, and are devoured by the beasts of the forest" (Mosiah 8:20–21; emphasis added).

A careful consideration of the characteristics of sheep helps us understand why a shepherd is so important. First and foremost, sheep as a species are preyed upon by various predators. Fortunately, sheep are also intensely social animals, which causes them to bond closely to other sheep in the flock. There is safety in numbers, and when threatened, they do one of two things: they either run from what frightens them, or they band together in tight, large groups for protection. It is harder for a predator—even the most vicious—to pick a sheep out of a group than to go after a few who have strayed from the

---

1   See also 1 Kings 22:17; 2 Chronicles 18:16.
2   See Psalm 119:176; Isaiah 53:6; Zechariah 13:7; Matthew 26:31; Mark 14:27; 1 Peter 2:25; Mosiah 14:6.

group. (And it is virtually impossible for a predator to conquer when a loving shepherd protects his flock.)

That flocking instinct can sometimes be to the sheep's detriment, especially when there is no shepherd to lead them. From birth, lambs learn to follow the older members of the flock—and when one sheep moves, the rest usually follow, even if it's not such a good idea. A powerful example illustrating the potential danger of the sheep's flocking and following instinct occurred in 2005 in eastern Turkey. Over four hundred sheep plunged to their deaths after one of their number tried to cross a deep ravine; the rest of the flock followed with tragic results.[3]

Sheep are most comfortable with their flock, and they will run as a group if they feel threatened or spooked. This is where the shepherd becomes so important: the sheep know his voice and follow him. Their instinct to follow their shepherd is even greater than the instinct to move with the flock. Modern-day shepherd Phillip Keller effectively described the importance of the shepherd based on his own experiences with his flock:

> In the course of time I came to realize that nothing so quieted and reassured the sheep as to see me in the field. The presence of their master and owner and protector put them at ease as nothing else could do. Continuous conflict and jealousy within the flock can be a most detrimental thing. The sheep become edgy, tense, discontented, and restless. They lose weight and become irritable. But one point that always interested me very much was that whenever I came into view and my presence attracted their attention, the sheep quickly forgot their foolish rivalries and stopped their fighting. The shepherd's presence made all the difference in their behavior.[4]

Elder Gerrit W. Gong taught that, as the "Shepherd of Israel" (Psalm 80:1), Jesus Christ exemplified the qualities shepherds possess. The Savior's example, he said, illustrates that good shepherds "must not slumber,[5] nor scatter or cause the sheep to go astray,[6] nor look [their] own way for [their] own gain.[7] . . . [Shepherds] are to strengthen, heal, bind up that which is broken, bring again that which was driven away, seek that which was lost."[8]

---

3 "Turkish Sheep Die in 'Mass Jump,'" *BBC News*, July 8, 2005, http://news.bbc.co.uk/2/hi/europe/4665511.stm.

4 W. Philip Keller, *A Shepherd Looks at Psalm 23*, (Grand Rapids, MI: Zondervan, 1970).

5 See Nahum 3:18.

6 See Jeremiah 23:1; 50:6, 44.

7 See Isaiah 56:11; Ezekiel 34:2–6.

8 Gerrit W. Gong, "Good Shepherd, Lamb of God," *Ensign* or *Liahona*, May 2019.

Sheep led by a shepherd quickly learn to trust the shepherd with their very lives. Most are familiar with the parable of the lost sheep[9] in which a shepherd, having a hundred sheep, leaves the ninety-nine to search for one that is lost. Archbishop Blase Cupich, Roman Catholic Archbishop of Chicago, told of a priest who once asked a shepherd if it was realistic for a shepherd to leave ninety-nine sheep in order to search for just one. The shepherd said that such a circumstance was absolutely realistic, "and when he returns the one to the fold, the other sheep realize that he will do the same for each of them, and as a result, they more tightly bond with the shepherd as one they trust."[10]

Our Savior, of course, is the ultimate example of a trustworthy shepherd as He "reaches out to the one and to the ninety-and-nine, often at the same time. . . . Our Lord seeks and delivers us 'out of all places,'[11] 'from the four quarters of the earth.'[12] He gathers us by holy covenant and His atoning blood."[13]

From these analyses, the shepherd's importance to the flock is clear. Their very lives depend on the wise and careful leadership of a good shepherd—and sheep that have no shepherd are left to their own weak devices, subject to predators and all manner of destruction.

In the same verse, Alma makes clear that he is addressing "workers of iniquity" who are "puffed up in the vain things of the world" and who, despite knowing "the ways of righteousness nevertheless have gone astray" (Alma 5:37). Interestingly, the phrase *puffed up* occurs in the New Testament[14] and in the Book of Mormon.[15] To be "puffed up in the vain things of the world" means to be selfishly fixated on things that are "empty; worthless; having no substance, value, or importance."[16]

In verse 37, Alma also condemns those of his listeners who "professed to have known the ways of righteousness." Prophets throughout the scriptures frequently indicted the covenant people for hypocrisy—for not practicing what they preached, for not doing that which they claimed to believe as true. Some of the first words of God the Father and Jesus Christ to Joseph Smith repeated one of Isaiah's prophecies: "They draw near to me with their lips, but their hearts

9   See Luke 15:4–6. Discussed in John W. Welch and Jeannie S. Welch, *The Parables of Jesus: Revealing the Plan of Salvation* (American Fork, Utah: Covenant Communications, 2019), 90–101.
10   Archbishop Blasé Cupich in Dias, *What Did Jesus Ask?* (New York: Time Inc. Books, 2015), 190–191.
11   Ezekiel 34:12.
12   1 Nephi 22:25.
13   See Hebrews 13:20; Gerrit W. Gong, "Good Shepherd, Lamb of God," *Ensign*, May 2019.
14   See 1 Corinthians 4:6, 18; 8:1; 13:4; Colossians 2:18.
15   See 2 Nephi 9:42; 28:9, 12–15; Alma 31:27; 3 Nephi 6:15; Moroni 7:45.
16   *Noah Webster's First Edition of an American Dictionary.*

are far from me, they teach for doctrines the commandments of men, having a form of godliness, but they deny the power thereof" (Joseph Smith— History 1:19; Isaiah 29:13).[17]

THERE ARE ONLY TWO FOLDS

Telling his listeners that they are like sheep that have gone astray, like sheep that have no shepherd, Alma then points out that "a shepherd hath called after you and is still calling after you, but ye will not hearken unto his voice!" (Alma 5:37). Just as only one of the two ways leads to eternal life in the celestial glory of God, so also only one shepherd leads the sheep to become members of his fold. In ancient times, the king was often referred to as the shepherd of his people, and that idea carried over into the biblical world. Psalm 23 begins, "The Lord [Jehovah] is my shepherd; I shall not want. He maketh me to lie down in green pastures: he leadeth me beside the still waters. He restoreth my soul: he leadeth me in the paths of righteousness for his name's sake. . . . And I will dwell in the house of the Lord for ever" (Psalm 23:1–3, 6). The Savior Himself declared that He had other sheep that needed to be brought into His fold, so that there would be "one fold and one shepherd" (3 Nephi 16:3).

For the prophet and priest Alma, that shepherd, of course, is the Good Shepherd—the Lord Jesus Christ. Alma emphasizes,

> Behold, I say unto you, that the good shepherd doth call you; yea, and in his own name he doth call you, which is the name of Christ; and if ye will not hearken unto the voice of the good shepherd, to the name by which ye are called, behold, ye are not the sheep of the good shepherd. (Alma 5:38)

It surely follows, then, that those who do not hearken to the voice of the Lord are not of His fold. And because there are only two folds, that leaves only one other option. In Alma's words, "Behold, I say unto you, that the devil is your shepherd, and ye are of his fold; and now, who can deny this? Behold, I say unto you, whosoever denieth this is a liar and a child of the devil" (Alma 5:39).

This is the only place in all of scripture that refers to Satan as a "shepherd." Alma described him thus for rhetorical reasons—to construct an elegant antithetical parallelism. Satan certainly does not have any shepherd-like qualities, for he "will not support his children at the last day, but doth speedily drag them down to hell" (Alma 30:60).

17   See also Psalm 28:3; Jeremiah 3:10; 9:8; 12:2; Ezekiel 33:30–33; Matthew 7:15; 15:8; Mark 7:6; Luke 6:46; 11:39; Titus 1:16; 2 Nephi 27:24–25; Mosiah 5:13; Alma 34:28.

In the same verse, Alma delivered a judgment that may seem unusually harsh when he called one who does not hearken to the Savior's voice "a liar and a child of the devil." Because Satan is "the father of all lies" (Moses 4:4), those who tell lies are, appropriately, his children:

> Just as we can take upon us the name of Christ and become the sons and daughters of God and heirs to his kingdom, so we can choose to take upon us the name of the adversary and become heirs of his kingdom. . . . Just as the people of Zion are eventually sealed to Christ (Mosiah 5:15), so the municipals of Babylon who deny and defy the truth shall eventually be sealed to Beelzebub (2 Nephi 9:46; Alma 34:35; Helaman 13:32).[18]

If we are not with the Lord's fold, then we are allied with the only other fold.

Alma was very stern with the people in Zarahemla because they had not been diligent enough in their faith in the Lord Jesus Christ.[19] Sometimes the Lord Himself speaks with a firm voice to help people realize their situation so they will not take lightly the words of His prophets. There are always two ways—two choices—in front of us. Lehi said it well:

> Wherefore, men are free according to the flesh; and all things are given them which are expedient unto man. *And they are free to choose liberty and eternal life, through the great Mediator of all men, or to choose captivity and death, according to the captivity and power of the devil;* for he seeketh that all men might be miserable like unto himself.
>
> And now, my sons, *I would that ye should look to the great Mediator, and hearken unto his great commandments; and be faithful unto his words, and choose eternal life, according to the will of his Holy Spirit;*
>
> And not choose eternal death, according to the will of the flesh and the evil which is therein, which giveth the spirit of the devil power to captivate, to bring you down to hell, that he may reign over you in his own kingdom. (2 Nephi 2:27–29; emphasis added)

18   Joseph F. McConkie and Robert L. Millet, *Doctrinal Commentary on the Book of Mormon*, (Salt Lake City: Bookcraft, 1991), 3:38.
19   See Alma 7:3.

We are always free to choose. If we do not choose the Lord, we become subject to the devil. There is no other way. The Lord Himself teaches, "I am the way, the truth, and the life: no man cometh unto the Father, but by me" (John 14:6). The scriptures provide numerous examples of those who chose something other than "the way, the truth, and the life." One of the most illustrative is Cain (as well as others of the children of Adam and Eve), who loved the devil more than God and became carnal, sensual, and devilish.[20] Cain became Perdition[21] and proclaimed, "Truly I am Mahan, the master of this great secret, that I may murder and get gain. Wherefore Cain was called Master Mahan, and he gloried in his wickedness" (Moses 5:31).

Giving even greater emphasis to the truth he was teaching, Alma said, "Therefore, if a man bringeth forth good works he hearkeneth unto the voice of the good shepherd, and he doth follow him; but whosoever bringeth forth evil works, the same becometh a child of the devil, for he hearkeneth unto his voice, and doth follow him" (Alma 5:41).

Alma was not alone in his denunciation of those who listen to the devil instead of the Lord. The Prophet Abinadi spoke strongly to those who choose the devil when he said,

> But remember that he that persists in his own carnal [sinful and unrepentant] nature, and goes on in the ways of sin and rebellion against God, remaineth in his fallen state and the devil hath all power over him. Therefore he is as though there was no redemption made, being an enemy to God; and also is the devil an enemy to God. (Mosiah 16:5)

Jesus Christ Himself described those who will not listen to His voice when He said to certain unbelieving Jews, "Ye are of your father the devil, and the lusts of your father ye will do. He was a murderer from the beginning, and abode not in the truth, because there is no truth in him. When he speaketh a lie, he speaketh of his own: for he is a liar, and the father of it" (John 8:44).

The flock with which we identify, the shepherd whose voice we follow, is of critical importance. For one thing, our "wages" are paid by the one we follow. As Alma pointed out with remarkable plainness, he who follows the devil as his shepherd "must receive his wages of [the devil]; therefore, for his wages he receiveth death, as to things pertaining unto righteousness, being dead unto all good works" (Alma 5:42).

---

20   See Moses 5:13, 28.
21   See Moses 5:24.

We receive entirely different wages from the Good Shepherd. In his momentous address to his people, King Benjamin outlined the blessings of aligning ourselves with the Lord as our shepherd:

> And now, because of the covenant which ye have made ye shall be called the children of Christ, his sons, and his daughters; for behold, this day he hath spiritually begotten you; for ye say that your hearts are changed through faith on his name; therefore, ye are born of him and have become his sons and his daughters.
>
> And under this head ye are made free, and there is no other head whereby ye can be made free. There is no other name given whereby salvation cometh; therefore, I would that ye should take upon you the name of Christ, all you that have entered into the covenant with God that ye should be obedient unto the end of your lives.
>
> And it shall come to pass that whosoever doeth this shall be found at the right hand of God, for he shall know the name by which he is called; for he shall be called by the name of Christ. . . .
>
> And I would that ye should remember also, that this is the name that I said I should give unto you that never should be blotted out, except it be through transgression; therefore, take heed that ye do not transgress, that the name be not blotted out of your hearts.
>
> I say unto you, I would that ye should remember to retain the name written always in your hearts, that ye are not found on the left hand of God, but that ye hear and know the voice by which ye shall be called, and also, the name by which he shall call you.
>
> For how knoweth a man the master whom he has not served, and who is a stranger unto him, and is far from the thoughts and intents of his heart?
>
> And again, doth a man take an ass which belongeth to his neighbor, and keep him? I say unto you, Nay; he will not even suffer that he shall feed among his flocks, but will drive him away, and cast him out. I say unto you, that even so shall it be among you if ye know not the name by which ye are called. (Mosiah 5:7–9, 11–14)

Building on King Benjamin's warning, Alma teaches another consequence of choosing the devil's flock when he says,

Their names shall be blotted out, that the names of the wicked shall not be numbered among the names of the righteous, that the word of God may be fulfilled, which saith: The names of the wicked shall not be mingled with the names of my people;

For the names of the righteous shall be written in the book of life, and unto them will I grant an inheritance at my right hand. And now, my brethren, what have ye to say against this? I say unto you, if ye speak against it, it matters not, for the word of God must be fulfilled. (Alma 5:57–58)

President Joseph Fielding Smith explained how critical it is to have our names written in the Lamb's Book of Life:

We are not going to be saved in the kingdom of God just because our names are on the records of the Church. It will require more than that. We will have to have our names written in the Lamb's Book of Life, and if they are written in the Lamb's Book of Life then it is an evidence we have kept the commandments. Every soul who will not keep those commandments shall have his name blotted out of that book.[22]

What exactly does the term *blotted out* mean?

Blotted out is used in two ways [in the King James Version of the Bible]. Sin or transgression is blotted out[23] and names or remembrances are blotted out from the book of life or from under heaven.[24] The Hebrew root here [of *blotted out*] is also translated as "put out" in Deut. 25:6 and "wiped out" in 2 Kgs. 21:13. Brigham Young explained that "We receive the Gospel, not that we may have our names written in the Lamb's book of life, but that our names may not be blotted out of that book."[25]

The Lord is the Good Shepherd. As King Benjamin declared, those of His fold are His disciples, His sons and daughters.[26] The use of this metaphor as a description of the Lord carries with it the love for His fold that only the Messiah

---

22   Joseph Fielding Smith, in Conference Report, Oct. 1950, 9–13.
23   See Nehemiah 4:5; Psalms 51:1, 9; Isaiah 43:25; 44:22; Jeremiah 18:23; Acts 3:19.
24   See Exodus 32:32–33; Deuteronomy 9:14; 25:19; 29:20; 2 Kings 14:27; Psalm 109:13; Colossians 2:14; Revelation 3:5. In Numbers 5:23, a curse is blotted out from a writing.
25   "Text, Notes, and Comments," in *King Benjamin's Speech: "That Ye May Learn Wisdom,"* eds. John W. Welch and Stephen D. Ricks (Provo, Utah: FARMS, 1998), 499.
26   See Mosiah 5:7.

would have.[27] The sheep know His voice,[28] and they are called in His own name—the name of Christ. In a revelation given to the Prophet Joseph Smith, the Lord said,

> Behold, Jesus Christ is the name which is given of the Father, and there is none other name given whereby man can be saved;
>
> Wherefore, all men must take upon them the name which is given of the Father, for in that name shall they be called at the last day;
>
> Wherefore, if they know not the name by which they are called, they cannot have place in the kingdom of my Father. (D&C 18:23–25)

Through baptism we testify that we are willing to take the name of Jesus Christ upon us.[29] Every Sabbath day when we partake of the sacrament, we renew the covenant to "witness unto thee, O God, the Eternal Father, that [we] are willing to take upon [us] the name of thy Son" (D&C 20:77).

HOW CHRIST TENDS HIS FLOCK

There is a significant difference between those who are hired to tend sheep—called *hirelings*—and those who are true shepherds. The Lord warns of hirelings, saying that they "careth not for the sheep" (John 10:13). Hirelings had to protect the sheep from being stolen from their presence,[30] but they could legally flee in the face of serious threat to the flock, saving their own lives but abandoning the helpless sheep to destruction, to be "torn in pieces" by wolves or other predators (Exodus 22:13). A true shepherd protects at any price, even that of his own life, the flock he owns and loves.

Alma's description of Christ as a shepherd verifies that He is a true shepherd: "For what shepherd is there among you having many sheep doth not watch over them, that the wolves enter not and devour his flock? And behold, if a wolf enter his flock doth he not drive him out? Yea, and at the last, if he can, he will destroy [the wolf]" (Alma 5:59).

The wolf metaphor was used by Christ in several different ways. Probably the best-known example is Christ's description of false prophets as those "who come to you in sheep's clothing, but inwardly they are ravening wolves" (3 Nephi 14:15).[31]

---

27 See Psalm 23; John 10:11, 14.
28 See John 10:27.
29 See D&C 20:37.
30 See Exodus 22:12.
31 See also Matthew 7:15; Acts 20:29; Alma 5:60.

In the New Testament, the devil and his followers are also described as wolves.[32] The wolf metaphor was used in the Old Testament to symbolize wicked rulers[33] or fierce enemies.[34] Isaiah employed the image of the wolf dwelling with the lamb to epitomize the nature of millennial existence.[35] Other than verses citing biblical passages, Alma's use of the wolf metaphor is more in keeping with the Old Testament notion of the wolf as a threatening enemy than the later notion of the wolf as a deceitful teacher.[36]

QUALIFYING FOR THE LORD'S FLOCK

Alma tells us that to qualify for the Lord's flock, we must bring forth good fruit:

> For I say unto you that whatsoever is good cometh from God, and whatsoever is evil cometh from the devil.
>
> Therefore, if a man bringeth forth good works he hearkeneth unto the voice of the good shepherd, and he doth follow him; but whosoever bringeth forth evil works, the same becometh a child of the devil, for he hearkeneth unto his voice, and doth follow him. (Alma 5:40–41)

By Alma's description, a disastrous outcome awaits those who do not bring forth good fruit. As directed by the Spirit, he proclaims,

> Behold, the ax is laid at the root of the tree; therefore every tree that bringeth not forth good fruit shall be hewn down and cast into the fire, yea, a fire which cannot be consumed, even an unquenchable fire. Behold, and remember, the Holy One hath spoken it. (Alma 5:52)

Alma is not the only one to use the imagery of being "hewn down" as a result of failing to do good works. In Zenos's allegory of the tame and wild olive trees, which is found in Jacob 5, the master of the vineyard works with his servants and invests exhaustive effort in planting and tending his vineyard. At the end, however, the master of the vineyard tells his servant,

> And now, behold, notwithstanding all the care which we have taken of my vineyard, the trees thereof have become corrupted,

---

32 See Matthew 10:16; Luke 10:3; John 10:12; Acts 20:29.
33 See Ezekiel 22:27; Zephaniah 3:3.
34 See Jeremiah 5:6; Habakkuk 1:8.
35 See Isaiah 11:6; 65:25.
36 See 3 Nephi 14:15.

that they bring forth no good fruit; and these I had hoped to
preserve, to have laid up fruit thereof against the season, unto
mine own self. But, behold, they have become like unto the
wild olive tree, and *they are of no worth but to be hewn down
and cast into the fire;* and it grieveth me that I should lose them.
(Jacob 5:46; emphasis added)

In His ministry to the Nephites on the American continent, the resurrected
Christ declared that any church not built upon His gospel

is built upon the works of men, or upon the works of the devil,
verily I say unto you they have joy in their works for a season,
and by and by the end cometh, and *they are hewn down and cast
into the fire,* from whence there is no return.

For their works do follow them, for *it is because of their works
that they are hewn down.* . . . (3 Nephi 27:11–12; emphasis added)

Alma also said that if we are to qualify for the Lord's flock, we must "come
. . . out from the wicked, and be . . . separate, and touch not their unclean
things" (Alma 5:57).

There are two ways of considering Alma's concern about unclean things. As
detailed in Leviticus 11, much of the law of Moses is dedicated to discerning
that which is "clean" from that which is "unclean." The Israelites were instructed
to abstain from certain foods and activities that fell into the "unclean" category.
As Alma's listeners were in the process of renewing their commitment to the law
of Moses, it is not surprising that he reminded them to refrain from touching
"unclean things."37

Another useful interpretation, especially for us in our day, is a more literal
meaning of the word *separate.* In an address at general conference, Elder
David R. Stone of the Seventy, who was involved in the construction of the
Manhattan New York Temple, talked about how wonderful it was "to sit in
the celestial room and be there in perfect silence, without a single sound to be
heard coming from the busy New York streets outside."38

Elder Stone wondered how it was possible that such reverence existed in
the temple when the noise of one of the nation's busiest metropolises was just a
few yards away. The answer, he said, "was in the construction of the temple. The
temple was built within the walls of an existing building, and the inner walls of

37   Compare Leviticus 5:2; 10:10; 13:3; 15:2, 31; Numbers 19:11; Judges 13:4; Job 14:4; Isaiah 35:8; 52:11;
     Ezekiel 44:23.
38   David R. Stone, in Conference Report, Apr. 2006, 94–97.

the temple were connected to the outer walls at only a very few junction points. That is how the temple . . . limited the effects of . . . the world outside."[39]

The lesson for us in that example, said Elder Stone, is limiting the extent to which the world around us influences our lives. We can, and should, remain separate. He concluded,

> Wherever we are, whatever city we may live in, we can build our own Zion by the principles of the celestial kingdom and ever seek to become the pure in heart. . . .
>
> We do not need to become as puppets in the hands of the culture of the place and time. We can be courageous and can walk in the Lord's paths and follow His footsteps.[40]

Part of separating ourselves from worldly influences is to keep ourselves focused on the Savior. In his general conference address in April 2017, President Russell M. Nelson challenged us to become powerful disciples by looking to Jesus Christ: "Our focus must be riveted on the Savior and His gospel. It is mentally rigorous to strive to look unto Him in *every* thought. But when we do, our doubts and fears flee."[41]

THE GOOD SHEPHERD NEVER STOPS CALLING TO US

Even as he singled out the "workers of iniquity" who were behaving as "sheep having no shepherd," Alma testified that "a shepherd hath called after you and is still calling after you" (Alma 5:37).

Contained in that statement is one of the most glorious truths about the Savior: regardless of what we have done, no matter who we are, whatever our circumstances, He will never stop calling us—never rescind His invitation to be part of His flock. Christ will continue to call His sheep—all of us—until that millennial day when "there is one God and one Shepherd over all the earth" (1 Nephi 13:41). For this reason, He is still calling and will call until the Millennium.

The concept of Christ as a shepherd originated in Old Testament times—He was "the shepherd, the stone of Israel" (see Genesis 49:24) long before He was "the good shepherd" of the New Testament.[42] Book of Mormon prophets often used shepherd imagery to portray Christ's care for each of us.[43] Alma is no exception. Immediately after telling his listeners that the Shepherd was still calling after them, Alma testifies, "Behold, I say unto you, that the good

39   David R. Stone, 94–97.
40   David R. Stone, 94–97.
41   Russell M. Nelson, "Drawing the Power of Jesus Christ into Our Lives," *Ensign* or *Liahona*, May 2017, 41.
42   See Psalms 23:1; 80:1; 95:7; Isaiah 40:11; Ezekiel 34:12; John 10; Hebrews 13:20; 1 Peter 2:25.
43   See 1 Nephi 22:25; Mosiah 26:21; Helaman 7:18; 15:13; 3 Nephi 15:21; 18:31; Mormon 5:17.

shepherd doth call you; yea, and in his own name he doth call you, which is the name of Christ; and if ye will not hearken unto the voice of the good shepherd, to the name by which ye are called, behold, ye are not the sheep of the good shepherd" (Alma 5:38).

Book of Mormon prophets knew the name of the coming Messiah.[44] Alma may have associated the imagery of the good shepherd with the idea of the Lord's name because of his father's influence. In a marvelous revelation that Alma the Elder recorded[45] soon after assuming responsibility for the Church in Zarahemla, the same connection was made by the Lord: "Yea, blessed is this people who are willing to bear my name; for in my name shall they be called; and they are mine . . . And they that will hear my voice shall be my sheep" (Mosiah 26:18, 21).

In Hebrew, the *name* "is sometimes used to signify the collected attributes or characteristics of the object named. This is particularly the case with the divine name, . . . where *name* embraces the whole divine nature revealed by the Son."[46] To take the Lord's name upon ourselves, then, is to cultivate His attributes in us, and to be called in His name means to be "purified even as he is pure" (Moroni 7:48), to be even as He is.

As he concludes his speech, Alma gives his listeners, then and now, a full measure of hope when he says,

> And now I say unto you that the good shepherd doth call after you; and if you will hearken unto his voice he will bring you into his fold, and ye are his sheep; and he commandeth you that ye suffer no ravenous wolf to enter among you, that ye may not be destroyed. (Alma 5:60)

As we keep our focus on the Savior, we can be assured that He will help us and guide us and bring us safely home. As we commit to that way of life, we should remember the words of Elder Joseph B. Wirthlin:

> As the clatter and clamor of life bustle about us, we hear shouting to "come here" and to "go there." In the midst of the noise and seductive voices that compete for our time and interest, a solitary figure stands on the shores of the Sea of Galilee, calling quietly to us, "Follow me."[47]

44   See 2 Nephi 10:3; 25:19, 24; 26:8; 31:10, 20; 33:4, 6; Mosiah 3:8; Alma 6:8.
45   See Mosiah 26:33.
46   Merrill F. Unger, *The New Unger's Bible Dictionary*, rev. ed., R. K. Harrison (Chicago: Moody Bible Institute of Chicago, 1957), 776.
47   Joseph B. Wirthlin, "Follow Me," *Ensign*, Apr. 2002.

CHAPTER SIX
BECOMING CLEAN THROUGH REPENTANCE

Behold, he sendeth an invitation unto all men, for the arms of mercy are extended towards them, and he saith: Repent, and I will receive you.
(Alma 5:33)

HAVING RECEIVED CHRIST'S IMAGE IN our countenance, and having been delivered from captivity and bondage, we want nothing more than to be received by Him, to go and be where He is. The Lord has made that possible through His infinite Atonement. But it is up to us to take advantage of His ultimate sacrifice by repenting.

In his October 1991 general conference address, Elder Neal A. Maxwell created a vivid image of repentance when he said, "Repentance requires both turning away from evil and turning to God. When 'a mighty change' is required, full repentance involves a 180-degree turn, and without looking back!"[1]

Exactly a decade later, he created another memorable image when he said, "But God does not have two sets of Ten Commandments, one indoor and another outdoor! Nor are there two approved roads to repentance. True, a weekend of regret may produce some 'sorrowing of the damned,' but not the 'mighty change' which only godly sorrow produces."[2]

President Ezra Taft Benson taught that an "important principle for us to understand if we would be true members of the Church is that repentance involves not just a change of actions, but a change of heart."[3]

Repentance, then, means "rethinking": it is the continuous, lifelong expansion of our minds so that our way of thinking eventually becomes indistinguishable from God's way of thinking.[4] Scholar Gary Gillum has said, "Repentance consists

---

1   Neal A. Maxwell, "Repentance," *Ensign,* Nov. 1991, 30.
2   Neal A. Maxwell, "The Seventh Commandment: A Shield," *Ensign,* Nov. 2001, 78.
3   C. Max Caldwell, "A Mighty Change," in *The Book of Mormon: Alma, the Testimony of the Word,* ed. Monte S. Nyman and Charles D. Tate Jr. (Provo, UT: Religious Studies Center, Brigham Young University, 1992), 27–46.
4   See Isaiah 55:8–9; Helaman 10:5.

not only of remorse, confession, restitution, and forgiveness, but a literal changing of one's entire perspective on life, so that eventually a Latter-day Saint may 'repent of having to repent.'"[5]

Calling upon God in prayer, doing all things in the name of the Son, and repenting have been the clarion call for all of God's children from the very beginning. Following the angel's explanation of why Adam was offering the sacrifices unto the Lord, the angel proceeded to give Adam the commandment to repent forevermore. "Wherefore, thou shalt do all that thou doest in the name of the Son, and thou shalt repent and call upon God in the name of the Son forevermore" (Moses 5:8).

Repentance is part of our daily activities, and on the Sabbath, we come with a broken heart and contrite spirit to partake of the sacrament, thus repenting by covenant with the Lord. One of the first four principles of the

ALMA'S QUESTIONS ON REPENTANCE

Can you withstand these sayings? (See Alma 5:53)

Can you lay aside these things and trample the Holy One under your feet? (See Alma 5:53)

Could you say that your garments have been cleansed and made white through the blood of Christ, who will come to redeem His people from their sins? (See Alma 5:27)

And now I ask of you, my brethren, how will any of you feel, if you shall stand before the bar of God, having your garments stained with blood and all manner of filthiness? (See Alma 5:22)

Behold, what will these things testify against you? (See Alma 5:22)

The names of the righteous shall be written in the book of life, and unto them will I grant an inheritance at my right hand. What have you to say against this? (See Alma 5:58)

gospel is repentance,[6] and it is essential for all of us. Our decisions and actions in mortality will testify against us if we do not experience a mighty change and take advantage of the Savior's Atonement to repent and become clean.

Look carefully at the teachings of all the prophets throughout recorded history; those teachings revolve around repenting, making a mighty change, and deepening our conversion. Prophets have called people to repentance since the beginning of time precisely because repentance is our lot—whether we are guilty of gross sins like the Nephites of Zarahemla or whether we are, relatively speaking, "in the

5 Gary P. Gillum, "Repentance Also Means Rethinking," in *By Study and Also by Faith*, eds. John M. Lundquist and Stephen D. Ricks (Salt Lake City: Deseret Book and FARMS, 1990), 2:406.
6 See Articles of Faith 4.

paths of righteousness" like the Gideonites—"for *all* have . . . come short of the glory," or intelligence,[7] "of God" (Romans 3:23; emphasis added).

Book of Mormon prophets were commanded to preach nothing but faith and repentance. As just one example, "Yea, even [Alma] commanded [the teachers and priests] that they should preach nothing save it were repentance and faith on the Lord, who had redeemed his people" (Mosiah 18:20). Alma wasn't alone in that emphasis; the principle of preaching and teaching faith and repentance is mentioned multiple times in the Book of Mormon.[8]

In our day, that's exactly what happens in every general conference: we exercise faith in the prophet's words and in the Lord and Savior Jesus Christ, and we accept the challenges and admonitions to repent. We work on making the necessary changes in our lives to be better disciples of the Lord Jesus Christ. We follow the counsel of our prophet, President Russell M. Nelson, who said, "To repent fully is to convert completely to the Lord Jesus Christ and His holy work. . . . That change comes when we are 'born again,' converted and focused upon our journey to the kingdom of God."[9]

In this last dispensation, the Lord similarly declared, "Say nothing but repentance unto this generation" (D&C 6:9). Indeed, the call to repentance resides at the center of all divinely inspired discourse, for "all men must repent" (2 Nephi 2:21). Commentators often dissect repentance into a formal, almost ritualistic, step-by-step process that must occur after the overt commission of sin. However, the Greek word *metaneō*, from which the word *repent* is translated in the King James Version of the Bible, denotes "a change of mind, i.e., a fresh view about God, about oneself, and about the world."[10]

God specifically proportioned this mortal existence to us so that we could "improve our time" (Alma 34:33) and "prepare to meet God" (Alma 12:24). Alma, in fact, defines mortality as "a space granted unto man in which he might repent" (Alma 12:24). Failing to use our time to achieve that aim, then, is tantamount to throwing away that time. It is no better than wasting our time in sin. Hugh Nibley put it this way:

> Sin is waste. It is doing one thing when you should be doing other and better things for which you have the capacity. . . . That is why even the righteous must repent, constantly and progressively, since all fall short of their capacity and calling.[11]

---

7   See D&C 93:36.

8   See Mosiah 2:12, 21; 18:7, 20; 25:15, 22; Alma 7:14; 9:27; 12:30; 22:14; 26:22; 34:17–18; 37:33; Helaman 6:4; 13:6; 15:7; 3 Nephi 7:16; 27:19; Moroni 3:3; 8:25.

9   Russell M. Nelson, "Repentance and Conversion," *Ensign* or *Liahona*, May 2007.

10   Bible Dictionary, "Repentance."

11   Hugh Nibley, "Zeal Without Knowledge," in *Nibley on the Timely and the Timeless*, ed. Truman G. Madsen (Provo, Utah: BYU Religious Studies Center, 1978), 1:264.

Speaking of the time we are to use in repenting, President Dallin H. Oaks said,

> The principle of restoration also means that persons who
> are not righteous in mortal life will not rise up righteous in
> the resurrection. Moreover, unless our mortal sins have been
> cleansed and blotted out by repentance and forgiveness, we
> will be resurrected with a "bright recollection" and a "perfect
> knowledge of all of our guilt, and our uncleanness." The
> seriousness of that reality is emphasized by the many scriptures
> suggesting that the resurrection is followed immediately by
> the Final Judgment. Truly, "this life is the time for men to
> prepare to meet God."[12]

At various times in his ministry, Alma graphically described the feelings he
had after being visited by the angel—a situation in which he fully understood
his sinful condition. Saying that he was "racked with eternal torment" and
"harrowed up to the greatest degree" (Alma 36:12), Alma reported that he was
"tormented with the pains of hell" (Alma 36:13) when he realized that he had
failed to keep the commandments—and, it might be argued that his situation
was even worse than failing to keep the commandments, for he had rebelled
against the Savior. Imagine the absolute agony he felt as he realized "so great
had been my iniquities, that the very thought of coming into the presence of
my God did rack my soul with inexpressible horror" (Alma 36:14). Saying he
suffered the pains of a damned soul,[13] he expressed the desire to "be banished
and become extinct both soul and body, that I might not be brought to stand
in the presence of my God to be judged of my deeds" (Alma 36:15).

The anguish is almost palpable. Contrast Alma's words with the final words
of the Book of Mormon confidently inscribed on the plates by the Prophet
Moroni: "I soon go to rest in the paradise of God, until my spirit and body shall
again reunite, and I am brought forth triumphant through the air, to meet you
before the pleasing bar of the great Jehovah, the Eternal Judge" (Moroni 10:34).

As we exercise faith unto repentance, our condition will become much
more like that of Moroni than that of Alma immediately following the angel's
visit. Ours can be one of mercy and safety instead of torment. Amulek taught,

> And thus he shall bring salvation to all those who shall believe on
> his name; this being the intent of this last sacrifice, to bring about
> the bowels of mercy, which overpowereth justice, and bringeth
> about means unto men that they may have faith unto repentance.

12   Dallin H. Oaks, "Resurrection," *Ensign*, May 2000, 14.
13   See Alma 36:16.

> And thus mercy can satisfy the demands of justice, and encircles them in the arms of safety, while he that exercises no faith unto repentance is exposed to the whole law of the demands of justice; therefore only unto him that has faith unto repentance is brought about the great and eternal plan of redemption.
>
> Therefore may God grant unto you, my brethren, that ye may begin to exercise your faith unto repentance, that ye begin to call upon his holy name, that he would have mercy upon you. (Alma 34:15–17)

Thus, Alma challenged his listeners to assess whether their garments were "stained with blood and all manner of filthiness" by sin, asking "Behold, what will these things testify against you?" (Alma 5:22). To them and to us, he taught that "no man can be saved except his garments are washed white; yea, his garments must be purified until they are cleansed from all stain" (Alma 5:21).

How are our garments cleansed and purified? Alma specified that such a process takes place "through the blood of him of whom it has been spoken by our fathers, who should come to redeem his people from their sins" (Alma 5:21). Repentance is the key: as Amulek told Zeezrom in the city of Ammonihah, "the Lord surely should come to redeem his people, but *that he should not come to redeem them in their sins, but to redeem them from their sins*" (Helaman 5:10; emphasis added).

Having our garments cleansed would indicate that we have been forgiven of our sins,[14] we are on the covenant path,[15] we are seeking to do good,[16] and we are doing our best to please our Heavenly Father.[17]

What are we willing to sacrifice to have our garments washed white? Ours needs to be the willingness expressed by King Lamoni's father when he said, "O God, Aaron hath told me that there is a God; and if there is a God, and if thou art God, wilt thou make thyself known unto me, and *I will give away all my sins* to know thee . . . and be saved at the last day" (Alma 22:18; emphasis added).

A WARNING: SPEEDILY REPENT

After talking about those who are plagued by pride and envy and who make a mock of their brother,[18] Alma boldly and clearly proclaims, "Wo unto

---

14 See D&C 58:42–43.
15 See 2 Nephi 9:41.
16 See Alma 7:24.
17 See John 8:28–29.
18 See Alma 5:28–30.

such an one, for he is not prepared, and the time is at hand that he must repent or he cannot be saved! Yea, even wo unto all ye workers of iniquity; repent, repent, for the Lord God hath spoken it!" (Alma 5:31–32).

It would not be the last time during his speech that he urged his listeners to speedily repent. To "all ye that will persist in your wickedness, I say unto you that these are they who shall be hewn down and cast into the fire except they speedily repent" (Alma 5:56).

The Old Testament provides valuable context for Alma's statement. In that day, people and their works were often described allegorically as trees and their fruits.[19] In the New Testament, John the Baptist and Christ Himself employed this allegorical imagery to distinguish between the righteous and the wicked.[20] And elsewhere in the Book of Mormon, prophets used the tree/fruit allegory extensively, teaching that the righteous bring those trees that bring forth good fruit and are preserved, while the wicked are those trees that bring forth evil fruit and are "hewn down and cast into the fire"[21]—a fire that cannot be consumed, even an unquenchable fire.

In Alma 5, Alma assures his listeners that the Spirit instructed him to preach repentance to them:

> Yea, *thus saith the Spirit*: Repent, all ye ends of the earth, for the kingdom of heaven is soon at hand; yea, the Son of God cometh in his glory, in his might, majesty, power, and dominion. Yea, my beloved brethren, I say unto you, that *the Spirit saith*: Behold the glory of the King of all the earth; and also the King of heaven shall very soon shine forth among all the children of men.
>
> And also *the Spirit saith unto me*, yea, crieth unto me with a mighty voice, saying: Go forth and say unto this people— Repent, for except ye repent ye can in nowise inherit the kingdom of heaven.
>
> And again I say unto you, *the Spirit saith*: Behold, the ax is laid at the root of the tree; therefore every tree that bringeth not forth good fruit shall be hewn down and cast into the fire, yea, a fire which cannot be consumed, even an unquenchable fire. Behold, and remember, the Holy One hath spoken it. (Alma 5:50–52; emphasis added)

---

19   See Psalm 1:3; Proverbs 11:30; Isaiah 61:3; 65:22; Jeremiah 17:8; Ezekiel 17:24.
20   See Matthew 3:10; 7:17–19; Luke 3:9; 6:43–44.
21   See Jacob 5:3–77; 6:7; Alma 32:37–43; 40:26; Helaman 14:18; 3 Nephi 14:19; 27:11–12, 17; Moroni 6:1.

Alma, speaking by the power of the Holy Ghost, proclaims and admonishes the people to repent, else they cannot inherit the kingdom of heaven. It is with a sense of urgency that Alma then speaks of the need to repent and bring forth good fruit, else they "shall be hewn down and cast into the fire" (Alma 5:52). Through all of it, Alma clearly reminds us that the Lord, "the Holy One hath spoken it" (Alma 5:52).

Why is it that in every dispensation the prophets have cried repentance? Because it is the prophet's responsibility to help people stay on the straight and narrow path, even the covenant path, so they can be worthy of all the promised blessings. The only way that can be accomplished is through preaching repentance.

In his October 1993 general conference address, Elder Spencer J. Condie related a true story that powerfully illustrates the importance of a warning voice:

> On a dark, rainy night in Tasmania in January 1975, a 7,300-ton barge smashed into two piers of the Tasman Bridge, which connects Hobart, Tasmania, with its eastern suburbs across the bay. Three spans of the bridge collapsed. An Australian family by the name of Ling were driving across the bridge when suddenly the bridge lights went out. Just then a speeding car passed them and disappeared before their very eyes. Murray Ling "slammed on his brakes and skidded to a stop, one yard from the edge of a black void."[22]
>
> Murray got his family out of the car and then began warning oncoming traffic of the disaster ahead. As he frantically waved his arms, to his horror, a car "swerved around him and plummeted into the abyss."[23] A second car barely stopped in time, but a third car showed no sign of slowing down and crashed into the Lings' car at the edge of the bridge.
>
> Suddenly a loaded bus headed toward Murray, ignoring his waving arms. In desperation, risking his very life, he "ran alongside the driver's window. 'There's a span missing,' he yelled."[24] The bus swerved just in time and came to a halt against the railing. Dozens of lives had been saved.[25]

Likening what happened on that Tasmanian bridge to the warnings our prophets give us, Elder Condie went on to say,

22   Stephen Johnson, "Over the Edge!" *Reader's Digest,* Nov. 1977, 128.
23   *Reader's Digest.*
24   *Reader's Digest.*
25   Spencer J. Condie, "A Mighty Change of Heart," *Ensign,* Nov. 1993.

I am grateful for these Brethren whom we sustain as prophets, seers, and revelators who forewarn us of bridges not to be crossed. These great men whom we sustain as prophets, seers, and revelators preach "not with enticing words of man's wisdom, but in demonstration of the Spirit and of power" (1 Cor. 2:4). Their motives are pure as they strive to build the kingdom of God and to uplift and edify the Saints of God. In the words of the Apostle Paul, they have become "prisoners of Christ" (see Eph. 3:1; Eph. 4:1; Philem. 1:1, 9; 2 Tim. 1:8), whose only desire is to do the Lord's will. Nothing more. Nothing less. And nothing else. *These are men of God!* May we heed their warning voices.[26]

AN INVITATION: "COME UNTO ME"

Speaking of the Savior, Alma tells his listeners, "Behold, he sendeth an invitation unto all men, for the arms of mercy are extended towards them, and he saith: Repent, and I will receive you" (Alma 5:33).

All men. Do we fully comprehend that? The Savior's invitation is extended to *all.* God is no respecter of persons. Every soul ever created can take full advantage of the Savior's Atonement, because it was performed for *all* of God's children. That means you. It means me. It means all of us.

Alma may have derived that wording from Nephi; in saying that there are none who cannot partake of the Savior's salvation, he wrote that the Savior

> hath given it free for all men; and he hath commanded his people that they should persuade all men to repentance. . . .
>
> [H]e inviteth them all to come unto him and partake of his goodness; and he denieth none that come unto him, black and white, bond and free, male and female; and he remembereth the heathen; and all are alike unto God, both Jew and Gentile. (2 Nephi 26:27, 33)

It is difficult for us to comprehend exactly what an incredible gift it is that the Lord has given us by enabling us to repent and be forgiven. President Boyd K. Packer testified, "The thought is this: the Atonement leaves no tracks, no traces. What it fixes is fixed. . . . The Atonement leaves no traces, no tracks. It just heals, and what it heals stays healed."[27]

---

26 Spencer J. Condie, "A Mighty Change of Heart," *Ensign*, Nov. 1993.
27 Boyd K. Packer, Address to the Seventy in General Conference Training Meeting, Apr. 7, 2015.

Alma spoke here of the Savior's arms of mercy.[28] The image of "the arm of the Lord" is a favorite of many Old Testament prophets, particularly Isaiah.[29] Nephi's unique predilection for the writings of Isaiah early in the Book of Mormon makes the image of "the arm of the Lord" a recurring one in the Book of Mormon as well, though it does not appear at all in the New Testament.[30]

What is the "arm of the Lord"? As one scholar wrote, the "arm of the Lord" is God's "extension of . . . power and compassion to us."[31] Elder Jeffrey R. Holland also interprets the arm of the Lord as God's loving extension of Himself into our lives: "God's arm is more than adequate. He can always claim and embrace the Israel that he loves."[32]

The extended arm is a bridge between two different beings. The arm of the Lord is an image that captures the condescension of an omnipotent, yet loving God touching our individual lives. From His exalted sphere, He reaches to our less-than-telestial sphere by virtue of "his holy arm" (Psalm 98:1).

Isaiah asks a probing question that sheds light on the arm of the Lord: "To whom is the arm of the Lord revealed?" (Isaiah 53:1). John S. Thompson and Eric Smith provide an important interpretation of this passage: "[This] question is often interpreted to mean that the arm of the Lord is revealed in the being of the mortal Messiah."[33]

The arm of God the Father, then, is appropriately the "one mediator between God and men, the man Christ Jesus" (1 Timothy 2:5). Christ is the arm that extends from the courts of celestial glory to "the lone and dreary world," "encircling" the souls of men in a redeeming embrace (2 Nephi 1:15; Mormon 6:17).

This interpretation squares with many of the other scriptural references to the arm of the Lord. First, Christ's very role as Mediator in the plan of redemption, as described above, supports the evidence that He is the "arm of the Lord"—He is consistently characterized as making "intercession between

---

28   See Alma 5:33.

29   See Isaiah 33:2; 40:10; 51:5; 52:10; 53:1; see also Exodus 15:16; Psalm 77:15.

30   For a comprehensive treatment of the occurrence of this image in the scriptures, see David Rolph Seely, "The Image of the Hand of God in the Book of Mormon and the Old Testament," in *Rediscovering the Book of Mormon*, eds. John L. Sorenson and Melvin J. Thorne (Salt Lake City: Deseret Book and FARMS, 1991), 140–150.

31   Dana M. Pike, "'How Beautiful upon the Mountains': The Imagery of Isaiah 52:7–10 and Its Occurrences in the Book of Mormon," in *Isaiah in the Book of Mormon*, eds. Donald W. Parry and John W. Welch (Provo, Utah: FARMS, 1998), 285.

32   Jeffrey R. Holland, "'More Fully Persuaded': Isaiah's Witness of Christ's Ministry," in *Isaiah in the Book of Mormon*, eds. Donald W. Parry and John W. Welch (Provo, Utah: FARMS, 1998), 11.

33   John S. Thompson and Eric Smith, "Isaiah and the Latter-day Saints: A Bibliographic Survey," in *Isaiah in the Book of Mormon*, eds. Donald W. Parry and John W. Welch (Provo, Utah: FARMS, 1998), 496. See also Hoyt W. Brewster Jr., *Isaiah, Plain and Simple: The Message of Isaiah in the Book of Mormon* (Salt Lake City: Deseret Book, 1995), 248; and Victor L. Ludlow, *Isaiah: Prophet, Seer, and Poet* (Salt Lake City: Deseret Book, 1982), 448.

God and men."[34] Nephi says that "the Lord God will proceed to make bare his arm in the eyes of all nations, in bringing about his covenants and his gospel unto those who are of the house of Israel" (1 Nephi 22:11), and we know from modern revelation that this "bringing about" of the covenants of God will be done by Christ, "the messenger of the covenant."[35] In other words, Christ, the arm of the Lord, will be revealed because it is He who will "bring about" the covenants of the gospel.

Finally, Isaiah testifies of God that "his arm shall rule for him" and "mine [God's] arms shall judge the people" (Isaiah 40:10; 51:5). Isaiah's testimony corresponds perfectly with John's testimony: "For the Father judgeth no man, but hath committed all judgment unto the Son . . . And hath given him authority to execute judgment also, because he is the Son of man" (John 5:22, 27).

Two parts of the observation of the Day of Atonement are reflected in the Savior's invitation, "Repent, and I will receive you" (Alma 5:33). Hugh Nibley said of the Day of Atonement ceremony, "*Teshuvah* is to return home; it's when you return and are let in. *Yashab* means to sit down beside your Lord. In one you return home, and in the other you enter the tent and sit down beside your Lord. . . . This is the imagery of the Atonement."[36] These two parts are reflected in the invitation: "Repent"—return home like the prodigal son—and "I will receive you"—"sit down in the kingdom of God, with Abraham, with Isaac, and with Jacob" (Alma 5:24).

The idea of "coming unto Christ" is prevalent in the scriptures. In a clever inversion of the frequently cited "knock and it shall be opened unto you" (Matthew 7:7), the Apostle John wrote, "Behold, I stand at the door, and knock: if any man hear my voice, and open the door, I will come in to him, and will sup with him, and he with me" (Revelation 3:20). Christ does not need to "come unto" each of us, for "he be not far from every one of us" (Acts 17:27); He is waiting at the door. But we need to "come unto" Him. The Apostle James stated it so well that the Lord echoed him in this dispensation: "Draw nigh unto God, and he will draw nigh to you" (James 4:8; D&C 88:63).

To "come unto the Lord God" or "come unto Christ" means to repent and receive mercy,[37] to humbly heed the Lord's command,[38] to deny oneself and take up the cross of discipleship,[39] to take part in His Church,[40] and to believe

---

34   Isaiah 53:12; Romans 8:34; Hebrews 7:25; 2 Nephi 2:9; Mosiah 15:8.
35   Malachi 3:1; Matthew 15:24; 3 Nephi 24:1; D&C 93:8.
36   Hugh Nibley, *Teachings of the Book of Mormon, Semester 2 Transcripts* (Provo, Utah: FARMS, 1993), 113.
37   See 2 Nephi 28:32; D&C 18:11.
38   See Exodus 24:1; Isaiah 55:3.
39   See Matthew 16:24; Mark 8:34; Luke 9:23; Moroni 10:32.
40   See D&C 10:67.

in Christ.[41] It also means to rest under Christ's "easy" yoke,[42] to "have life" and never hunger (John 5:40), to come unto the Father, and to be "perfected in Christ" (Moroni 10:32). In short, it means that our will, like Christ's will, must be "swallowed up in the will of the Father," and consequently, all our afflictions will be "swallowed up in the joy of Christ" (Alma 31:38).

True repentance brings unspeakable joy because we become clean through the blood of the Lamb.[43] In Alma 36, Alma describes his experience of becoming clean with these descriptive words: "And oh, what joy, and what marvelous light I did behold; yea, my soul was filled with joy as exceeding as was my pain! . . . Yea, and again I say unto you . . . [that] there can be nothing so exquisite and sweet as was my joy" (Alma 36:20–21).

The Lord's joy is great over the soul that repents,[44] and we likewise feel joy. Bringing souls to repentance was Alma's great joy:

> I know that which the Lord hath commanded me, and I glory in it. I do not glory of myself, but I glory in that which the Lord hath commanded me; yea, and this is my glory, that perhaps I may be an instrument in the hands of God to bring some soul to repentance; and this is my joy.
>
> And behold, when I see many of my brethren truly penitent, and coming to the Lord their God, then is my soul filled with joy; then do I remember what the Lord has done for me, yea, even that he hath heard my prayer; yea, then do I remember his merciful arm which he extended towards me. (Alma 29:9–10)

Alma said that those of us who desire to follow our beloved Savior need to separate ourselves from the wicked and not even touch unclean things.[45] While such counsel might seem unusually harsh, this doctrine was taught from the beginning when Adam and Eve were commanded, "But of the fruit of the tree [of good and evil] which thou beholdest in the midst of the garden, God hath said—Ye shall not eat of it, *neither shall ye touch it,* lest ye die" (Moses 4:9; emphasis added). Additionally, we are told to avoid even the appearance of evil.[46]

The Savior's invitation to come unto Him is not an empty one. The Good Shepherd is our friend; He is always there for us in all things.[47] As the Good

---

41   See Hebrews 11:6.
42   See Matthew 11:28–30.
43   See Mormon 9:6.
44   See D&C 18:13.
45   See Alma 5:57.
46   See 1 Thessalonians 5:22.
47   See D&C 84:88.

Shepherd, He has given His life for us.[48] He is a personal Savior who knows our names.[49] As our Advocate[50] and Mediator,[51] He makes intercession for us all.[52] We are told of Him, "Greater love hath no man than this, that a man lay down his life for his friends. Ye are my friends, if ye do whatsoever I command you" (John 15:13–14).[53]

With gratitude, Alma concludes his masterful discourse with these compelling words:

> And now I say unto you that the good shepherd doth call after you; and if you will hearken unto his voice he will bring you into his fold, and ye are his sheep; and he commandeth you that ye suffer no ravenous wolf to enter among you, that ye may not be destroyed.
>
> And now I, Alma, do command you in the language of him who hath commanded me, that ye observe to do the words which I have spoken unto you.
>
> I speak by way of command unto you that belong to the church; and unto those who do not belong to the church I speak by way of invitation, saying: Come and be baptized unto repentance, that ye also may be partakers of the fruit of the tree of life. (Alma 5:60–62)

Of the Savior's steadfast loyalty to us, Elder Allen D. Haynie said,

> I testify that the Savior will never turn away from us when we humbly seek Him in order to repent; will never consider us to be a lost cause; will never say, "Oh no, not you again"; will never reject us because of a failure to understand how hard it is to avoid sin. He understands it all perfectly, including the sense of sorrow, shame, and frustration that is the inevitable consequence of sin.[54]

The Lord is forever calling after us to bring us safely home if we will but hearken to His voice.

48   See John 10:11.
49   See John 10:3.
50   See 1 John 2:1.
51   See 2 Nephi 2:27–28.
52   See 2 Nephi 2:9.
53   See also D&C 84:63, 77.
54   Allen D. Haynie, "Remembering in Whom We Have Trusted," *Ensign* or *Liahona*, Nov. 2015.

CHAPTER SEVEN
STANDING BEFORE GOD AT THE JUDGMENT DAY

I say unto you, can you imagine to yourselves that ye hear the voice of the Lord, saying unto you, in that day: Come unto me ye blessed, for behold, your works have been the works of righteousness upon the face of the earth? (Alma 5:16)

THE MIDDLE PART OF ALMA's speech—the part concerning eternal judgment—is the most scathing indictment of those in his audience, then and now, who fail to repent and walk an undeterred course on the covenant path. By using a dozen provocative questions, Alma tries to prompt his listeners to imagine where they will be at the judgment day—an exercise not likely previously entertained by many of them. It is probable that Alma was using this approach to move his listeners toward righteousness.

As we examine his questions and the things Alma tries to impress on his listeners, it is clear that we are judged according to our deeds in the flesh—and that there are only two eventual outcomes. President Russell M. Nelson put it very plainly in a description of what we will each be expected to do at that day:

> Although your spirit had a veil of forgetfulness placed over it at the time of your birth into mortality, it retained its power to remember all that happens—precisely recording each event of life. Indeed, scriptures warn "that every idle word that men shall speak, they shall give account thereof in the day of judgment." Prophets refer to our "bright recollection" and "perfect remembrance" at that day of decision.[1]

---

1   Russell M. Nelson, "Self-Mastery," *Ensign*, Nov. 1985, 30.

ALMA'S QUESTIONS ON PREPARING FOR THE JUDGMENT

Do you view this mortal body raised . . . to stand before God to be judged according to the deeds which have been done in the mortal body? (See Alma 5:15)

Can you imagine to yourself that you hear the voice of the Lord, saying unto you, in that day: Come unto me blessed, for behold, your works have been works of righteousness upon the face of the earth? (See Alma 5:16)

Or do you imagine to yourself that you can lie unto the Lord in that day, and say—Lord, my works have been righteous works upon the face of the earth—and that He will save you? (See Alma 5:17)

Or otherwise, can you imagine yourself brought before the tribunal of God with your soul filled with guilt and remorse, having a remembrance of all your guilt, yea, a perfect remembrance of all your wickedness, yea, a remembrance that you have set at defiance the commandments of God? (See Alma 5:18)

Can you look up to God at that day with a pure heart and clean hands? (See Alma 5:19)

Can you look up, having the image of God engraven upon your countenance? (See Alma 5:19)

Can you think of being saved when you have yielded yourself to become subject to the devil? (See Alma 5:20)

How will you feel if you shall stand before the bar of God, having your garments stained with blood and all manner of filthiness? (See Alma 5:22)

What will these things testify against you? (See Alma 5:22)

Will they not testify that you are a murderer? (See Alma 5:23)

Will they not also testify that you are guilty of all manner of wickedness? (See Alma 5:23)

Do you suppose that such an one can have a place to sit down in the kingdom of God, with Abraham, with Isaac, and with Jacob, and also all the holy prophets, whose garments are cleansed and are spotless, pure and white? (See Alma 5:24)

Reeling with that "bright recollection," we will be expected to account to the Lord for the things for which we have not repented. In that way, we will testify against ourselves—but in the final analysis, our decisions and actions in mortality will also testify against us if we do not experience a mighty change and take advantage of the Savior's Atonement to repent and become clean.

These dozen questions concern the state of the individual's soul at the final judgment day. Alma wishes to impress upon his audience that there are ultimately only two possible outcomes at the final judgment: eternal joy or eternal remorse. Those who are righteous will have the image of God upon their countenances and will be found spotless and pure; others will be stained and unfit for the presence of God. This dualistic conception, or the doctrine of the Two Ways, is discussed throughout the Book of Mormon—the wicked and the righteous, the broad path to the devil and the straight and narrow path to eternal life (the covenant path), consequences of sin and blessings for righteousness. The vivid belief that all people will someday stand before God to give an accounting and to be judged is a powerful motivator of moral behavior.[2]

HOW THE FINAL JUDGMENT WORKS

We learn in the scriptures what happens in the Final Judgment. During that experience, we will stand before what Moroni calls "the pleasing bar of the great Jehovah, the Eternal Judge of both quick and dead" (Moroni 10:34).[3]

One of the most important things we learn is that our *natures* do not magically change, and our works in the flesh will factor into our judgment in a substantial way. Jacob taught that in the Final Judgment, "they who are righteous shall be righteous still, and they who are filthy shall be filthy still" (2 Nephi 9:16).[4] What that means, according to Alma, is that God's justice requires that "all things should be restored to their proper order" (Alma 41:2). In other words, "if [our] works were good in this life, and the desires of [our] hearts were good, . . . at the last day, [we will] be restored unto that which is good" (Alma 41:3). The opposite holds true: "if [our] works [or our desires] are evil [we] shall be restored [to] them for evil" (Alma 41:4–5).[5]

Clearly, repentance is essential. But the *timing* of our repentance may be just as important as the act itself. President Dallin H. Oaks said,

---

2   The previous paragraph was adapted from John W. Welch and J. Gregory Welch, *Charting the Book of Mormon* (Provo, Utah: FARMS, 1999), Chart 63.

3   See also Jacob 6:9–13; 3 Nephi 27:16.

4   See also 1 Nephi 15:33; Mormon 9:14.

5   See also Helaman 14:31.

To assure that we will be clean before God, we must repent *before* the Final Judgment (see Mormon 3:22). As Alma told his sinful son, we cannot hide our sins before God, "and *except ye repent* they will stand as a testimony against you at the last day" (Alma 39:8; emphasis added). The Atonement of Jesus Christ gives us the only way to achieve the needed cleansing through repentance, and this mortal life is the time to do it.[6]

President Oaks went on to teach that even though some repentance can happen in the spirit world,[7] such repentance is not as certain. According to Elder Melvin J. Ballard, "It is much easier to overcome and serve the Lord when both flesh and spirit are combined as one. This is the time when men are more pliable and susceptible. . . . This life is the time to repent."[8]

When we repent prior to the Final Judgment, the Lord assures us that we are cleansed. Our sins—including any sinful desires we had—are forgiven, and the Lord in His mercy will "remember them no more" (D&C 58:42).[9] Thus cleansed through repentance, we can qualify for eternal life, described by King Benjamin as "dwell[ing] with God in a state of never-ending happiness" (Mosiah 2:41).

ONE OF TWO OUTCOMES: A SOUL FILLED WITH GUILT AND REMORSE

Alma is direct and straightforward in asking his listeners two pointed questions:

> [D]o ye imagine to yourselves that ye can lie unto the Lord in that day, and say—Lord, our works have been righteous works upon the face of the earth—and that he will save you?
>
> Or otherwise, can ye imagine yourselves brought before the tribunal of God with your souls filled with guilt and remorse, having a remembrance of all your guilt, yea, a perfect remembrance of all your wickedness, yea, a remembrance that ye have set at defiance the commandments of God? (Alma 5:17–18)

---

6   Dallin H. Oaks, "Cleansed by Repentance," *Ensign* or *Liahona*, May 2019.
7   See D&C 138:31, 33, 58.
8   Melvin J. Ballard, *Melvin J. Ballard: Crusader for Righteousness* (Salt Lake City: Bookcraft, 1966), 212–213.
9   See also Isaiah 1:18; Jeremiah 31:34; Hebrews 8:12; Alma 41:6; Helaman 14:18–19.

No one can lie to the Lord. It simply cannot be done, because the Lord knows the thoughts and the intents of our heart.[10] In his masterful sermon on the Lord's Atonement, Jacob made the consequence for lying very clear when he taught, "Wo unto the liar, for he shall be thrust down to hell" (2 Nephi 9:34). Moroni explained the plight of those who think they can lie and be blessed in vivid language when he said,

> Behold, I say unto you that ye would be more miserable to dwell with a holy and just God, under a consciousness of your filthiness before him, than ye would to dwell with the damned souls in hell.
>
> For behold, when ye shall be brought to see your nakedness before God, and also the glory of God, and the holiness of Jesus Christ, it will kindle a flame of unquenchable fire upon you. (Mormon 9:4–5)

There are examples in the scriptures of people who tried to lie to the Lord, and they paid a horrible price. In one of the most severe cases, Ananias and his wife, Sapphira, sold a piece of land so they could give the money to the Church. But when Ananias gave the Apostle Peter the money, he held part of it back, "his wife also being privy to it" (Acts 5:2).

Peter, discerning what Ananias had done, asked why Satan had filled his heart "to lie to the Holy Ghost, and to keep back part of the price of the land" (Acts 5:3). Peter then proclaimed, "thou hast not lied unto men, but unto God. And Ananias hearing these words fell down, and gave up the ghost: and great fear came on all them that heard these things" (Acts 5:4–5). Ananias was carried out and buried.

Three hours later, Sapphira arrived, not knowing what had happened. Peter directly asked her if the money Ananias gave him represented the full amount they had received for the land. Party to the deception, she said it was. Peter then said,

> How is it that ye have agreed together to tempt [test or try] the Spirit of the Lord? behold, the feet of them which have buried thy husband are at the door, and shall carry thee out.
>
> Then fell she down [immediately] at his feet, and yielded up the ghost: and the young men came in, and found her dead, and, carrying her forth, buried her by her husband. (Acts 5:9–10)

---

10   See Alma 18:32.

Alma refers to being brought before "the tribunal of God." This appears to be the only time that the word *tribunal* is used in all of scripture. According to Webster, a *tribunal* is "the seat of a judge or one acting as a judge."[11] The words *bar*,[12] *throne*,[13] and *judgment-seat*[14] are generally used to denote the same idea. We can understand, then, that "the tribunal of God" is the seat upon which God sits as our judge. As a judge, Alma no doubt saw people who stood before him as plaintiffs, defendants, or witnesses, trying to claim that their actions had been legal, when they knew full well that they were not. He can thus well imagine how pointless it would be to try to fool the Lord God Himself, the Eternal Judge who knows all things.

According to Alma, the punishment of the wicked is simple: "souls filled with guilt and remorse, having a remembrance of all your guilt, yea, a perfect remembrance of all your wickedness, yea, a remembrance that ye have set at defiance the commandments of God" (Alma 5:18). He is not the only prophet to have made such a statement. Moroni said the wicked will be "racked with a consciousness of guilt that [they] have ever abused [God's] laws" (Mormon 9:3).[15] Jacob said we will have a "perfect knowledge of all our guilt, and our uncleanness, and our nakedness" when we appear before the judgment bar.[16]

Alma recounted his own sins and feelings of remorse:

> Yea, I did remember all my sins and iniquities, for which I was tormented with the pains of hell; yea, I saw that I had rebelled against my God, and that I had not kept his holy commandments.
>
> Yea, and I had murdered many of his children, or rather led them away unto destruction; yea, and in fine so great had been my iniquities, that the very thought of coming into the presence of my God did rack my soul with inexpressible horror.
>
> Oh, thought I, that I could be banished and become extinct both soul and body, that I might not be brought to stand in the presence of my God, to be judged of my deeds. (Alma 36:13–15)

---

11   *Webster's Third New International Dictionary* ed., Philip Babcock Gove (Massachusetts: Merriam-Webster, 1961), 2441.

12   See 2 Nephi 33:11; Jacob 6:9, 13; Mosiah 16:10; Alma 11:44; Mormon 9:13; Moroni 10:27, 34.

13   See Psalm 9:7; Matthew 19:28; Luke 22:30; 1 Nephi 12:9–10; 2 Nephi 28:23.

14   See Romans 14:10; 1 Nephi 10:21; 2 Nephi 9:15; 33:7, 15; 3 Nephi 28:31; Mormon 3:20, 22; 6:21; 7:6; Ether 12:38; Moroni 8:20–21.

15   See also Isaiah 59:12; 2 Nephi 9:14; Mosiah 3:25; Alma 11:43; Mormon 9:4–6.

16   See 2 Nephi 9:14.

Thanks to the Savior's magnificent Atonement, we are assured that regardless of our sins, we can be spared this kind of agony if we fully repent. As Alma described it, the guilt of sins is a horrible state of being, which is why the penitent express so much gratitude when their sins are swept away.[17] As one example, Enos experienced the blessing of having his guilt swept away because of his faith in the Lord Jesus Christ when he was forgiven of his sins.[18] The Doctrine and Covenants gives us hope and peace of mind when the Lord said, "Behold, he who has repented of his sins, the same is forgiven, and I, the Lord, remember them no more. By this ye may know if a man repenteth of his sins—behold, he will confess them and forsake them" (D&C 58:42–43).

Alma then asks his listeners, "I say unto you, can ye think of being saved when you have yielded yourselves to become subjects to the devil?" (Alma 5:20). During mortality, we must choose to subject ourselves either to God or to Satan; there is no neutral territory, as many have supposed. If we are not "anxiously engaged" in God's cause, then we have "yielded [our]selves to become subjects to the devil"—and Satan wins by default. President Henry B. Eyring taught,

> Men and women have falsely argued from the beginning of time that to take counsel from the servants of God is to surrender God-given rights of independence. But the argument is false because it misrepresents reality. When we reject the counsel which comes from God, we do not choose to be independent of outside influence. We choose another influence . . . In rejecting His counsel, we choose the influence of another power, whose purpose is to make us miserable and whose motive is hatred. We have moral agency as a gift from God. Rather than the right to choose to be free of influence, it is the unalienable right to submit ourselves to whichever of those powers we choose.[19]

How do we yield ourselves to become subject to the devil? Rebelling against the truth and pridefully seeking our will instead of the will of God demonstrate the attributes of those who have subjected themselves to the devil. Mormon described some other key characteristics:

> But whatsoever thing *persuadeth men to do evil*, and *believe not in Christ*, and *deny him*, and *serve not God, then ye may know with a perfect knowledge it is of the devil;* for after this manner doth the devil work, for he persuadeth no man to do good,

---

17 See Enos 1:6–8; Alma 24:10; D&C 58:42–43.

18 See Enos 1:6–8.

19 Henry B. Eyring, "Finding Safety in Counsel," *Ensign,* May 1997, 25.

no, not one; neither do his angels; *neither do they who subject themselves unto him.* (Moroni 7:17; emphasis added)

In discussing those who are subject to the devil, Alma used an interesting phrase when he said that no man "can be saved except his garments are washed white; yea, his garments must be purified until they are cleansed from all stain, through the blood of him of whom it has been spoken by our fathers, who should come to redeem his people from their sins" (Alma 5:21).

Covenant people have always worn sacred garments, which began when "the Lord God, [made] coats of skins and clothed" Adam and Eve (Moses 4:27); covenant people still wear garments in our dispensation.[20] The very wearing of the garment distinguished the covenant people from the rest of the world; the proper wearing and condition of the garment distinguished the "valiant" among the covenant people from the merely "honorable."[21]

Elder Carlos E. Asay wrote, "How one wears the garment is the expression of how the individual feels about the Church and everything that relates to it. It is a measure of one's worthiness and devotion to the gospel."[22] Quoting a letter from the First Presidency, Elder Asay called the garment "an outward expression of an inward commitment," postulating that "Our very salvation depends, symbolically, upon the condition of our garments."

Alma often employs garment imagery as a metaphor for personal worthiness,[23] and many other prophets, both from the Book of Mormon and the Bible, did the same.[24] Indeed, the condition of the holy garments is often used as a metaphor for our readiness for salvation. Those with garments "washed white . . . cleansed from all stain, through the blood [of Christ]" (Alma 5:21) will be "purified even as [Christ] is pure" (Moroni 7:48) and thus will be worthy to abide in His presence.

Alma teaches his listeners that their garments could be cleansed from all stain through the blood of Jesus Christ. This paradoxical image of blood cleansing blood—the blood of the Lamb cleansing "the blood of this wicked generation" (D&C 88:75)—possessed more than mere symbolic value to those who practiced the law of Moses. It's an image that emerged from an actual Day of Atonement ritual. Hugh Nibley explained,

---

20   See Exodus 28:1–3; Revelation 3:4–5; Moses 7:3.
21   See D&C 76:75, 79.
22   Carlos E. Asay, "The Temple Garment: 'An Outward Expression of an Inward Commitment,'" *Ensign*, Aug. 1997.
23   See Alma 5:21, 24; 13:10–13; 34:36.
24   See Ecclesiastes 9:8; Isaiah 52:1; 61:10; Daniel 7:9; Matthew 22:2–14; Luke 24:4; Jude 1:23; Revelation 16:15; 1 Nephi 12:10; 2 Nephi 8:24; 9:14; Jacob 1:19; 2:2; Mosiah 2:27–28; 3 Nephi 19:25; 27:19; Mormon 9:35; Ether 12:37; 13:10.

When he [the priest] cuts the throat of the beast he becomes completely spattered with blood. . . . When the priest and his sons come out, having performed the sacrifice, their garments are spattered with this blood. That blood testifies that the sacrifice has been made, and the other garments are washed clean . . . by the blood of the Lamb. It testifies that they have been cleansed. . . . these symbols were very real to these people. . . . It's the Lamb's blood on the garment of the high priest that makes your garment white."[25]

Alma continues to use the symbolic aspect of garments in his next question: "And now I ask of you, my brethren, how will any of you feel, if ye shall stand before the bar of God, having your garments stained with blood and all manner of filthiness? Behold, what will these things testify against you?" (Alma 5:22).

Why do garments get stained with blood to begin with? For the house of Israel, "the life of the flesh is in the blood" (Leviticus 17:11). Being "stained with blood" means that one has taken the life of others. This may denote physical murder, but it also functions as a metaphor for spiritual murder. Nibley provided another explanation:

[Alma] says the blood will testify against you. We are guilty of what we assent to. We may not have shed very much blood, but we are all guilty of what we assent to. We all pay the same half shekel. It's very interesting that everybody must pay a sin tax, a tax for sin, on the Day of Atonement. But the interesting point is you don't know how to valuate sin. Who is more guilty than the other? There's no way of knowing how guilty a person really is. So everybody must pay.[26]

The "blood of this wicked generation" (D&C 88:75) is upon our garments because, though we may not actively participate, we often assent to or allow what others do.

The only way to "wash" garments that are stained and filthy is to repent. Those who fully repent and are truly forgiven have their garments washed white; those who fail to do so have garments that remain unclean. Alma describes the feeling of being unclean and not forgiven:

---

25 Hugh Nibley, *Teachings of the Book of Mormon, Semester 2 Transcripts* (Provo, Utah: FARMS, 1993), 286.
26 *Teachings of the Book of Mormon,* 285.

But I was racked with eternal torment, for my soul was harrowed up to the greatest degree and racked with all my sins.

Yea, I did remember all my sins and iniquities, for which I was tormented with the pains of hell; yea, I saw that I had rebelled against my God, and that I had not kept his holy commandments.

Yea, and I had murdered many of his children, or rather led them away unto destruction; yea, and in fine so great had been my iniquities, that the very thought of coming into the presence of my God did rack my soul with inexpressible horror.

Oh, thought I, that I could be banished and become extinct both soul and body, that I might not be brought to stand in the presence of my God, to be judged of my deeds.

And now, for three days and for three nights was I racked, even with the pains of a damned soul. (Alma 36:12–16)

What will a stained garment testify against us? A stained garment is a result of a life of unrepented sins. The phrase "having your garments stained with blood and all manner of filthiness" depicts a horrible state of sin and the feelings of the unrepentant. Jacob described this concept to those he taught so he would not have their blood on his garments:

O, my beloved brethren, remember my words. Behold, I take off my garments, and I shake them before you; I pray the God of my salvation that he view me with his all-searching eye; wherefore, ye shall know at the last day, when all men shall be judged of their works, that the God of Israel did witness that I shook your iniquities from my soul, and that I stand with brightness before him, and am rid of your blood. (2 Nephi 9:44)

And we did magnify our office unto the Lord, taking upon us the responsibility, answering the sins of the people upon our own heads if we did not teach them the word of God with all diligence; wherefore, by laboring with our might their blood might not come upon our garments; otherwise their blood would come upon our garments, and we would not be found spotless at the last day. (Jacob 1:19)

Alma then boldly proclaims that stained and filthy garments "testify that ye are murderers, yea, and also that ye are guilty of all manner of wickedness" (Alma 5:23).

Were the Church members in Zarahemla really murderers? For that matter, are *we* really murderers? In this passage, Alma seems to be speaking in terms of spiritual rather than physical death, as he did in describing his past transgressions to his son, Helaman: "Yea, and I had murdered many of his children, *or rather led them away unto destruction*" (Alma 36:14; emphasis added). Likewise, the wickedness of the Church in Zarahemla had become a "great stumbling-block to those who did not belong to the church" (Alma 4:10), leading people away rather than ushering them into the fold of God.

Alma is not referring to taking another's physical life, then, but rather is referring to the destruction or devastation of one's soul. It is the act of leading others astray—or, like King Noah, being the cause of another's life of sin. This is why Alma and the sons of King Mosiah were so anxious to repair the damage[27] they had done to the Church in leading so many astray.[28] This is why Jacob took his responsibility as a teacher so seriously[29]—he felt responsible for those he was teaching. In the same vein, parents are responsible for teaching their children, or else they become accountable for their children's sins.[30]

Before any of us feel vindicated because we have not physically murdered anyone, we need to recognize that spiritual murder is much more destructive than physical murder. The Savior Himself said, "Fear not them which kill the body, but are not able to kill the soul: but rather fear him which is able to destroy both soul and body in hell" (Matthew 10:28).

While murder has been specified in this part of Alma's discourse as a sin, there are many additional ways in which we can sin and stain our garments. King Benjamin mentioned that he could not number all the ways of sin.[31] That is why we seek to repent; that is why we come with a broken heart and contrite spirit to partake of the sacrament each week. We are forever in the process of deepening our conversion through repentance.

Alma concludes his discussion of the consequences of having filthy, stained garments—a manifestation of unrepented-for sin—by asking the following:

> Behold, my brethren, do ye suppose that such an one can have a
> place to sit down in the kingdom of God, with Abraham, with

---

27 See Alma 36:14.
28 See Mosiah 27:32–37.
29 See Jacob 1:19; 2:2.
30 See D&C 68:25.
31 See Mosiah 4:29.

Isaac, and with Jacob, and also all the holy prophets, whose garments are cleansed and are spotless, pure and white?

I say unto you, Nay; except ye make our Creator a liar from the beginning, or suppose that he is a liar from the beginning, ye cannot suppose that such can have place in the kingdom of heaven; but they shall be cast out for they are the children of the kingdom of the devil. (Alma 5:24–25)

"To 'sit down' with these ancient worthies [Abraham, Isaac, and Jacob] is to qualify for their company, to be confident and at ease in their presence, and to receive exaltation and godhood, for that is the condition and state of these patriarchs."[32] Alma provides a metaphor for obtaining eternal life, for it is associated with a wide variety of other metaphors for eternal life, such as "sitting at the right hand of God,"[33] "sitting down in the kingdom of God,"[34] "sitting down with Abraham," or in other words, taking one's place among the gods.[35] Christ's eternal glory is represented as sitting down "upon the throne of his glory,"[36] "on the throne of his power,"[37] and "on the right hand of the Father."[38]

We all understand that no unclean thing can dwell with God. Nephi taught, "Wherefore, if ye have sought to do wickedly in the days of your probation, then ye are found unclean before the judgment-seat of God; and no unclean thing can dwell with God; wherefore, ye must be cast off forever" (1 Nephi 10:21).[39] Thus, we understand the importance of repentance unto salvation as the only way to become free from sin.

The temple teaches precious truths about exaltation. Our judgment is not about our stations, possessions, and callings; it is about our personal righteousness. Teaching the people in Gideon, Alma makes this doctrinal point very clear:

And see that ye have faith, hope, and charity, and then ye will always abound in good works.

And may the Lord bless you, and keep your garments spotless, that ye may at last be brought to sit down with

---

32   Joseph F. McConkie and Robert L. Millet, *Doctrinal Commentary on the Book of Mormon* (Salt Lake City: Bookcraft, 1991), 3:56.
33   See Psalm 110:1; Matthew 22:44; 26:64; Mark 12:36; 14:62; Luke 20:42; 22:69; Acts 2:34; Hebrews 1:13.
34   See Alma 29:17.
35   See Matthew 8:11; Luke 13:29.
36   See Psalm 47:8; Matthew 25:31.
37   See D&C 76:108.
38   See Mark 16:19; Colossians 3:1; Hebrews 1:3; 10:12; Moroni 7:27; D&C 20:24.
39   See also 1 Nephi 15:34; Alma 5:57; 7:21; 11:37; 40:26; Helaman 8:25; 3 Nephi 27:19.

Abraham, Isaac, and Jacob, and the holy prophets who have been ever since the world began, having your garments spotless even as their garments are spotless, in the kingdom of heaven to go no more out. (Alma 7:24–25)

THE OTHER OUTCOME: "COME UNTO ME, YE BLESSED"

In providing the specifics of the other outcome, Alma asked,

Do ye exercise faith in the redemption of him who created you? Do you look forward with an eye of faith, and view this mortal body raised in immortality, and this corruption raised in incorruption, to stand before God to be judged according to the deeds which have been done in the mortal body?

I say unto you, *can you imagine to yourselves* that ye hear the voice of the Lord, saying unto you, in that day: Come unto me ye blessed, for behold, your works have been the works of righteousness upon the face of the earth? (Alma 5:15–16; emphasis added)

Notice that Alma asks us to *imagine*. Hugh Nibley taught,

[I]s it legitimate to imagine? Are you cheating if you imagine too much? Is all that we have of the gospel just imagination? Are we just making it up? We think it's very real to us. . . . You can imagine you hear the voice of the Lord. Before you can carry out any operation, you must visualize it. You must imagine it, no matter what it's going to be. So there's nothing wrong with imagining things—you have to.[40]

Recognize the importance of being able to forecast and to think, *What's it going to be like when we stand before God to be accounted, to be judged according to the deeds that we've done in this mortal body?* Can you imagine yourself on that occasion hearing the voice of the Lord saying to you in that day, "Come unto me ye blessed, for behold your works have been works of righteousness upon the face of the earth"?

Alma explained another aspect to achieving the reality of that vision when he asked, "I say unto you, can ye look up to God at that day with a pure heart and clean hands? I say unto you, can you look up, having the image of God engraven upon your countenances?" (Alma 5:19).

40   Hugh Nibley, *Teachings of the Book of Mormon, Semester 2 Transcripts* (Provo, Utah: FARMS, 1993), 283.

[This] question is a reminder that our souls are both physical and spiritual (D&C 88:15) and both need to be free from sin. . . . We are all responsible for controlling our physical bodies and behaving in accordance with standards of righteousness. . . . Some think and express the idea that they are powerless to change the innate desires of their flesh. . . . [But] the Lord expects all of us to subdue our environment and control its effect upon our souls. . . . The covenant people are required to subdue their flesh and thus have "clean hands." . . .

Clean hands reflect pure thoughts and internal conditions and are symbolized by the phrase *pure of heart*. No act was ever performed that did not originate as a thought in the mind. If we control our minds, we will control our bodies. What we do is predicated upon what we are. . . . People with clean hands and pure hearts are those who have the "image of God engraven upon [their] countenances." (Alma 5:19)[41]

In Hebrew thought, the word *hand* (Hebrew *yad* or *kap*) possessed rich symbolic value: "Hands are the symbols of human actions; *pure* hands represent pure actions and *unjust* hands injustice."[42] President Dallin H. Oaks said concerning clean hands, "If we do righteous acts and refrain from evil acts, we have clean hands."[43]

Alma's penetrating question brings the reality of a pure and clean life to the forefront of the mind. A pure heart is uncontaminated, unpolluted, untainted, unsullied, and uncorrupted. Indeed, a pure heart is without guile, pride, and any form of duplicitous feelings. Our motives are virtuous and free from any deceitfulness. We will be able to ascend the hill of the Lord, His holy temple, and there enjoy the presence and blessings of the Lord.[44]

How can we be completely pure and virtuous when we are still mortal and subject to sin? The answer is that we can aspire to absolute purity in the strength of the Lord and through the help of the Spirit. We can repent and practice spiritual endurance.

Purity of heart is reflected in our behavior, our thoughts, our intentions, and through our affections toward God. When we have a change of heart and

---

41   C. Max Caldwell, "A Mighty Change," in *Alma, the Testimony of the Word*, eds. Monte S. Nyman and Charles D. Tate (Provo: Religious Studies Center, 1992), 39–40.

42   Merrill F. Unger, *The New Unger's Bible Dictionary*, rev. ed. (Chicago: Moody Bible Institute of Chicago, 1957), 446.

43   Dallin H. Oaks, *Pure in Heart* (Salt Lake City: Bookcraft, 1988), 1.

44   See Psalm 24:3–5.

follow through with a change in the way we comport ourselves—cultivating a "godly walk and conversation" (D&C 20:69)—we become pure and receive the blessings of the Spirit, being worthy to be in the presence of God.[45]

We should control our minds and think of good and virtuous things. Thoughts dwelled upon create a desire that, if encouraged, results in action. This is why we are commanded to "let virtue garnish [our] thoughts unceasingly" (D&C 121:45). There is great power in worthy mental exertion that activates faith! We are commanded to think about just, pure, and lovely things and to practice virtue and holiness before the Lord.[46]

Jacob encouraged us with these words, directed to those who are pure in heart: "Look unto God with firmness of mind, and pray unto him with exceeding faith, and he will console you in your afflictions. . . . O all ye that are pure in heart, lift up your heads and receive the pleasing word of God, and feast upon his love; for ye may, if your minds are firm, forever" (Jacob 3:1–2).

If we are faithful in keeping the commandments, we will express the desire of coming before the great Jehovah to be judged, just as Moroni did when he said, "And now I bid unto all, farewell. I soon go to rest in the paradise of God, until my spirit and body shall again reunite, and I am brought forth triumphant through the air, *to meet you before the pleasing bar of the great Jehovah*, the Eternal Judge of both quick and dead. Amen" (Moroni 10:34; emphasis added).

Can you imagine how Alma felt when the Lord said, "Thou art my servant; and I covenant with thee that thou shalt have eternal life; and thou shalt serve me and go forth in my name, and shalt gather together my sheep" (Mosiah 26:20). What a glorious concept that gives us motivation to keep the commandments[47] and go about doing good.[48]

In His perfect plan, God always includes promised blessings with all commandments and covenants. If we are faithful in keeping the commandments, we are promised blessings in all things, both temporal and spiritual, and we will be able to dwell with God in never-ending happiness.[49]

If we receive the Holy Ghost and continue to be worthy of His presence and power, we have been promised a multiplicity of blessings from and by the power of the Holy Ghost. If we receive the greater priesthood and the ordinances and covenants in the temple, we can receive the Father's kingdom and all that our Father has.[50]

---

45 See Matthew 5:8.
46 See D&C 46:33.
47 See Mosiah 2:41.
48 See Alma 7:24.
49 See Mosiah 2:41.
50 See D&C 84:35–39.

If we are faithful in all things, we can take part in the first resurrection of the just, because we have received a testimony of our Savior Jesus Christ, have received the ordinances of the gospel, and have become clean through Christ the Lord by the power of the Holy Ghost. We have become part of the Church of the Firstborn. The Father will have given us all things. We become kings and queens to the Most High God and receive of His glory. We will glory in God and dwell in His and our Savior's presence. We will be just men and women made perfect through Christ the Lord, and we will enter into the promised glory of the celestial kingdom.[51] We will become gods and will receive eternal life.[52]

REQUIREMENTS FOR THOSE WHO ENTER GOD'S KINGDOM

In his discourse, Alma mentions a handful of attributes necessary for those who enter God's kingdom.

Stripped of Pride
Alma asks,

ALMA'S QUESTIONS ON REQUIREMENTS FOR GOD'S KINGDOM

Are you stripped of pride?
(See Alma 5:28)

Is there one among you who is not stripped of envy? (See Alma 5:29)

Can you be puffed up in the pride of your heart? (See Alma 5:53)

Will you still persist in the wearing of costly apparel and setting your heart upon the vain things of the world, upon your riches? (See Alma 5:53)

Is there one among you that doth make a mock of his brother, or that heapeth upon him persecution? (See Alma 5:30)

Will you persist in supposing that you are better than another? (See Alma 5:54)
Will you persist in the persecution of your brethren, who humble themselves and do walk after the holy order of God, wherewith they have been brought into this church having been sanctified by the Holy Spirit, and they do bring forth works which are meet for repentance? (See Alma 5:54)

Will you persist in turning your back upon the poor and needy, and in withholding your substance from them? (See Alma 5:55)

Have ye walked, keeping yourselves blameless before God? Could ye say, if ye were called to die at this time, within

---

51   See D&C 76:50–70.
52   See D&C 132:19–20.

yourselves, that ye have been sufficiently humble? That your garments have been cleansed and made white through the blood of Christ, who will come to redeem his people from their sins? (Alma 5:27)

According to Book of Mormon theology, there are three classes of people who will be found "blameless before God": little children,[53] those who are ignorant or "without the law,"[54] and those who are "perfected in Christ" (Moroni 10:32) by obedience to the principles and ordinances of the gospel.[55] In order to stand blameless before God, we need to be perfected in Christ. Moroni tells us how:

> Yea, come unto Christ, and be perfected in him, and deny yourselves of all ungodliness; and if ye shall deny yourselves of all ungodliness, and love God with all your might, mind and strength, then is his grace sufficient for you, that by his grace ye may be perfect in Christ; and if by the grace of God ye are perfect in Christ, ye can in nowise deny the power of God.
>
> And again, if ye by the grace of God are perfect in Christ, and deny not his power, then are ye sanctified in Christ by the grace of God, through the shedding of the blood of Christ, which is in the covenant of the Father unto the remission of your sins, that ye become holy, without spot. (Moroni 10:32–33)

As we come unto Christ with full purpose of heart and follow Him, we become His disciples and can become like Him.[56] We take up our cross (our burdens and afflictions) and follow Him through all exigencies.[57] We give our all to the Lord.

Alma challenges us to assess our standing if we were "called to die at this time" (Alma 5: 27). What a sobering assumption. When we are called to die, what regrets will we have? For what will we want just a little more time?

Alma asks if we are sufficiently humble. "The Hebrew word that most nearly describes the state of humility required to put off the natural man is *sepel ruah*, 'lowly of spirit' (see Proverbs 16:19; 29:23). In Greek only one

---

53   See Mosiah 3:16, 21; 15:25; Moroni 8:12–13, 19–23.
54   See 2 Nephi 9:25–26; Mosiah 3:11; 15:24; Alma 29:5; 42:16–22.
55   See 2 Nephi 9:23–24; Mosiah 3:21; 15:22; Moroni 10:32–34.
56   See Matthew 11:28–30; 3 Nephi 27:20; D&C 93:1.
57   See Matthew 16:24; 19:21; John 10:27; 12:26; 2 Nephi 31:12–13.

word is used for being humble, *tapeinos*, also meaning 'lowly of spirit.'"[58] Elder Neal A. Maxwell offered a keen definition of humility:

> Humility is not the disavowal of our worth; rather, it is the sober realization of how much we are valued by God. Nor does true humility call for the denigration of what truth we already know; rather, it is the catching of one's breath, as he realizes how very little that which we mortals presently know really is.[59]

Humility is the beginning virtue of all spiritual growth. When we understand and acknowledge our relationship to and dependence on God, we begin to be humble. In the state of humility—being submissive, easily entreated, and teachable—we receive the blessings of humility, including peace, inspiration, hope, and the guidance of the Lord. Humility involves having a broken heart and a contrite spirit, and it causes one to relate to God in gratitude and love.

Humility provokes us to pray, an act demonstrating we know our dependence and relationship to God the Father. Humility gives us strength in the Lord. This strength gives us self-worth and the self-confidence to do significant things. President Ezra Taft Benson taught,

> With humility, there come many blessings. For example, 'Be thou humble; and the Lord thy God shall lead thee by the hand, and give thee answer to thy prayers' (D&C 112:10). The humble will 'be made strong, and blessed from on high, and receive knowledge' (D&C 1:28). The Lord is 'merciful unto those who confess their sins with humble hearts' (D&C 61:2). Humility can turn away God's anger (see Helaman 11:11).[60]

What of pride? Alma asked, "Behold, are ye stripped of pride? I say unto you, if ye are not ye are not prepared to meet God. Behold ye must prepare quickly; for the kingdom of heaven is soon at hand, and such an one hath not eternal life" (Alma 5:28).

Hugh Nibley taught that being stripped of pride "means you put your pride off. . . . Pride is [displayed in] costly apparel . . . We're stripped of pride [with our white] garment."[61] Moroni specified that to be "stripped of

58   John W. Welch and Stephen D. Ricks, eds., *King Benjamin's Speech: "That Ye May Learn Wisdom"* (Provo, Utah: FARMS, 1999), 564.

59   Neal A. Maxwell, *The Neal A. Maxwell Quote Book* (Salt Lake City: Bookcraft, 1997), 165.

60   *The Teachings of Ezra Taft Benson* (Salt Lake City: Bookcraft, 1988), 370.

61   Hugh Nibley, *Teachings of the Book of Mormon, Semester 2 Transcripts* (Provo, Utah: FARMS, 1993), 290.

pride" means to be "stripped" of "costly apparel," which reveals our humble garments or our "nakedness before God" (Mormon 9:5–6).

Pride is often called "the universal sin" because it is at the crux of almost every other sin. Pride is expressed in arrogance, haughtiness, self-love, vanity, and egotism. Because pride involves man setting his will against God's, it creates enmity between God and man. In the Book of Mormon, pride was the downfall of the Jaredite and Nephite peoples, and pride can be our downfall as well if we are not careful. Prideful thoughts are so powerful that they can lead to sinful thoughts and behaviors, such as selfishness, greed, lust, jealousy, power-seeking, envy, and a whole host of related sins—which is exactly why the Lord continually counsels us against pride.[62]

Pride separates us from God and is directly opposed to the Christlike quality of humility. Just as the spacious building in Lehi's dream had no foundation,[63] those who separate themselves from God have no foundation. They are left to themselves, and their pride will be their downfall, for they will receive no strength from God in pride.

On April 1, 1989, President Ezra Taft Benson delivered his landmark sermon on pride:

> Essentially, pride is a "my will" rather than "thy will" approach to life. The opposite of pride is humbleness, meekness, submissiveness, or teachableness (see Alma 13:28). . . . Pride does not look up to God and care about what is right. It looks sideways to man and argues who is right. Pride is manifest in the spirit of contention. Was it not through pride that the devil became the devil? Christ wanted to serve. The devil wanted to rule. Christ wanted to bring men to where He was. The devil wanted to be above men. Christ removed self as the force in His perfect life. It was not my will, but thine be done (see Mark 14:36; Luke 22:42). . . . [Pride] is self-will as opposed to God's will. It is the fear of man over the fear of God.[64]
>
> [Pride] is manifest in so many ways, such as faultfinding, gossiping, backbiting, murmuring, living beyond our means, envying, coveting, withholding gratitude and praise that might lift another, and being unforgiving and jealous. . . . The antidote for pride is humility—meekness, submissiveness.

62   See Proverbs 16:18; D&C 23:1.

63   See 1 Nephi 8:26.

64   *The Teachings of Ezra Taft Benson* (Salt Lake City: Bookcraft, 1988), 435.

We can choose to humble ourselves by conquering enmity towards our brothers and sisters, . . . by receiving counsel and chastisement, . . . by forgiving those who have offended us, . . . by rendering selfless service, . . . by going on missions and preaching the word that can humble others, . . . by getting to the temple more frequently, . . . [and] by confessing and forsaking sins and being born of God.[65]

After asking his listeners if they are stripped of pride, Alma asks, "can ye lay aside these things, and trample the Holy One under your feet; yea, can ye be puffed up in the pride of your hearts; yea, will ye still persist in the wearing of costly apparel and setting your hearts upon the vain things of the world, upon your riches?" (Alma 5:53).

"Trampling the Holy One under your feet" seems to be a stock element of prophetic indictment in the Book of Mormon. Disregard of the Lord and His commandments is often referred to as an act of "trampling under one's feet."[66]

Alma asks if his listeners, then and now, set their hearts upon their riches. Christ wisely instructed all would-be disciples, "Wherefore, settle this in your hearts, that ye will do the things which I shall teach, and command you" (JST Luke 14:27–28). To follow Christ, we must set or settle our hearts first upon doing His will and entering His kingdom, not upon accumulating riches.[67] This phrase seems to originate in one of David's psalms: "If riches increase, *set not your heart upon them*" (Psalm 62:10; emphasis added). This psalm's sentiment is echoed throughout the book of Proverbs.[68] One Bible dictionary adds this insight:

> In the Bible, material goods are generally esteemed as gifts of God, received through God's blessing (Deut. 28:1–14). . . . many biblical writers note a tendancy for the wealthy to exploit the poor (Isa. 3:13–26; James 5:1–6) or at least fail to assist the poor in a manner befitting those who love their neighbors as themselves (cf. Lev. 19:18). According to Moses, the wealthy were expected to exercise generosity in helping to meet the needs of the poor (Deut. 15:10). . . . Wealth is not to be sought for its own sake (Prov. 28:20, 22).[69]

65   Ezra Taft Benson, "Beware of Pride," *Ensign*, May 1989, 4.
66   See 1 Nephi 19:7; Mosiah 29:21–22; Alma 60:33; Helaman 4:21–22; 12:2; 3 Nephi 28:35. For use of the phrase in other books of holy writ, see Matthew 7:6; D&C 3:15.
67   See Jacob 2:18.
68   See Proverbs 11:4, 28; 13:7; 22:1, 16; 23:4; 27:24.
69   *HarperCollins Bible Dictionary*, 3rd rev. updated ed. (New York: HarperOne, 2011), 1096–1097.

Jacob counseled, "And after ye have obtained a hope in Christ ye shall obtain riches, if ye seek them; and ye will seek them for the intent to do good—to clothe the naked, and to feed the hungry, and to liberate the captive, and administer relief to the sick and the afflicted" (Jacob 2:19).

The Lord's counsel has always been to seek the riches of eternity rather than the riches of this world,[70] for "the love of money is the root of all evil" (1 Timothy 6:10). In the Book of Mormon, the arrogant striving for treasures upon earth instead of treasures in heaven resulted in both intermittent punishments[71] and ultimate destruction.[72]

It should be noted that certain Book of Mormon authors distinguish between the mere *possession* of riches and the unrighteous *love* of riches,[73] but the tragic reality of Book of Mormon events overwhelmingly demonstrates the improbability of people righteously managing material wealth, for "at the very time when [the Lord] doth prosper his people . . . they do harden their hearts, and do forget the Lord their God . . . because of their ease, and their exceedingly great prosperity" (Helaman 12:2). The phrase is extensively used throughout the Book of Mormon to indicate oncoming apostasy.[74]

Stripped of Envy

Alma's next question concerns another characteristic that could keep us from entering the kingdom of God: "Behold, I say, is there one among you who is not stripped of envy? I say unto you that such an one is not prepared; and I would that he should prepare quickly, for the hour is close at hand, and he knoweth not when the time shall come; for such an one is not found guiltless" (Alma 5:29). It is interesting to note that envy follows pride in Alma's catalogue of sins, for "he is proud, knowing nothing . . . whereof cometh envy" (1 Timothy 6:4).

The Hebrew word translated as envy—*qin'a*—originally meant "a burning, then the colour produced in the face by a deep emotion, thus ardour, zeal, jealousy. . . . Envy creates sorrow that others have what we have not."[75] The final commandment in the Ten Commandments prohibits the righteous from coveting or envying anything that a neighbor might have.

---

70 See D&C 38:39.
71 See Helaman 13:21–23.
72 See Helaman 13:31–38.
73 See Jacob 2:18–19; Alma 62:49.
74 See Mosiah 12:29; Alma 1:30; 5:53; Helaman 6:17; 7:21; 12:4; 13:20.
75 *The New Bible Dictionary*, 3rd ed., I. Howard Marshall, A. R. Millard, J. I. Packer, and D. J. Wiseman, eds. (Downers Grove, Illinois: InterVarsity Press, 1996), 334. Compare Proverbs 14:30; 24:1; Isaiah 11:13; Matthew 27:18; Acts 7:9; 13:45; 17:5; Romans 13:13; 1 Corinthians 3:3; 13:4; Galatians 5:21; 1 Timothy 6:4; Titus 3:3; James 3:16; 4:5; 2 Nephi 26:21, 32; Alma 1:32; 4:9; 16:18; Helaman 13:22; 3 Nephi 30:2; 4 Nephi 1:16; Mormon 8:28, 36; D&C 101:6; 127:2.

Alma cautions us immediately concerning the devastating effects of envy and our need to prepare to meet God by being stripped of all envy. Envy is one of the unseen cancers of sin, complicating life to a degree that it leads to other sins. Envy also leads to jealousy, discontent, greed, covetousness, resentment, and bitterness. It destroys good will, feelings of well-being, and happiness.

With envy, self-perception is skewed, resulting in the desire to have more and be more than someone else. Envy can escalate over a multitude of things—money, status, relationships, physical appearance, apparent success, or fame. Self-generated, envy is considered one of the deadly sins. Consuming in nature, it often begins with the fatal practice of comparison and has no place in a Christ-centered life.

Elder Jeffrey R. Holland said,

> It has been said that envy is the one sin to which no one readily confesses, but just how widespread that tendency can be is suggested in the old Danish proverb, "If envy were a fever, all the world would be ill." . . . As others seem to grow larger in our sight, we think we must therefore be smaller. So, unfortunately, we occasionally act that way.
>
> How does this happen, especially when we wish so much that it would not? I think one of the reasons is that every day we see allurements of one kind or another that tell us what we have is not enough. Someone or something is forever telling us we need to be more handsome or more wealthy, more applauded or more admired than we see ourselves as being. We are told we haven't collected enough possessions or gone to enough fun places. We are bombarded with the message that on the *world's* scale of things we have been weighed in the balance and found wanting. . . .
>
> But God does not work this way. . . .
>
> I testify that no one of us is less treasured or cherished of God than another. I testify that He loves each of us—insecurities, anxieties, self-image, and all. He doesn't measure our talents or our looks; He doesn't measure our professions or our possessions. He cheers on *every* runner, calling out that the race is against sin, *not* against each other. I know that if we will be faithful, there is a perfectly tailored robe of righteousness ready and waiting for *everyone*, "robes . . . made

. . . white in the blood of the Lamb." May we encourage each other in our effort to win that prize.[76]

Overcoming envy begins with the knowledge of our divine heritage and an understanding that God is no respecter of persons. Heavenly Father loves all His children and seeks for everyone's happiness through righteousness, and it matters not that one is further down the covenant path. We cheer for all and love all in their pursuit of happiness in and through the gospel of Jesus Christ and the Lord's Infinite Atonement.

How We Treat Others

Alma then shifts his questioning to the way in which we treat others:

> And again I say unto you, is there one among you that doth make a mock of his brother, or that heapeth upon him persecutions?
>
> Wo unto such an one, for he is not prepared, and the time is at hand that he must repent or he cannot be saved! (Alma 5:30–31)

We are told that to mock is

> to humiliate, ridicule, insult, revile, make fun of, deride, sneer at, scorn, or hold in contempt. . . . Occasions for mockery usually occur in the context of real or imagined differences. Differences in beliefs, wealth, learning, social position, physical characteristics, group membership, and behavior, may be used as pretexts for the justification of mockery. . . . Mockery costs our brother or sister severe physical and/or psychological pain. It also jeopardizes our hope of eternal life. Moreover, it is especially debilitating to those who have been called to serve. We cannot serve those for whom we have contempt.[77]

It's hard to completely escape mockery. Sadly, there's a lot of teasing and bullying in elementary schools, so many children grow up with it. We need to be very careful as parents and in our families that we do not ever tear anyone down. As Professor Robert K. Thomas often taught, "Scoffing often takes on the appearance of valid criticism. . . . If we indulge this temptation to ridicule, we

---

76 Jeffrey R. Holland, "The Other Prodigal," *Ensign*, May 2002, 63–64.
77 Gary L. Bunker, "Mocking Our Brother," *Ensign*, Apr. 1975, 36, 37, 41.

can easily substitute jeering and emotional tirade for thoughtful consideration."[78] People who mock know that damage is done, and there's really no way the victim can answer, let alone recover.

Alma identified the attitude that in turn causes mockery:

> Yea, will ye persist in supposing that ye are better one than another; yea, will ye persist in the persecution of your brethren, who humble themselves and do walk after the holy order of God, wherewith they have been brought into this church, having been sanctified by the Holy Spirit, and they do bring forth works which are meet for repentance. (Alma 5:54)

Tragically, people have left the Church over feeling belittled or mocked, believing that others feel superior to them; as a result, they feel they are not valued. The Lord gave all of us the following injunction: "But I say unto you, Love your enemies, bless them that curse you, do good to them that hate you, and pray for them which despitefully use you, and persecute you" (Matthew 5:44).[79]

The Lord warns those who persecute the meek: "they persecute the meek, and their hearts are upon their treasures; wherefore, their treasure is their god. And behold, their treasure shall perish with them also" (2 Nephi 9:30).[80]

President Dallin H. Oaks said,

> This is a potent reminder that neither riches nor lineage nor any other privileges of birth should cause us to believe that we are "better one than another" (Alma 5:54; see also Jacob 3:9). Indeed, the Book of Mormon commands, "Ye shall not esteem one flesh above another, or one man shall not think himself above another" (Mosiah 23:7).[81]

Finally, Alma asks, "Yea, and will you persist in turning your backs upon the poor, and the needy, and in withholding your substance from them?" (Alma 5:55).

Alma chastised the people for withholding their substance from the poor and needy because it was a widespread practice in Zarahemla prior to the time

78 Robert K. Thomas, Academic Vice President at Brigham Young University, often made this point in his honors classes at BYU in the 1960s. Quote from Daryl R. Hague, ed., *A Love of Learning: Speeches of Robert K. Thomas* (Provo: BYU Studies, 2011), 174, building on Alexander Pope, *An Essay on Criticism*, who warns against our "itching to deride."
79 See also 3 Nephi 12:44.
80 See also 2 Nephi 28:13; Jacob 2:13.
81 Dallin H. Oaks, "All Men Everywhere," *Ensign* or *Liahona*, May 2006.

Alma left the judgment seat.[82] As a result, it was fresh on his mind when he delivered the strong admonitions in his discourse.

The Lord is very firm concerning helping the poor and needy and reminds us with this warning: "Therefore, if any man shall take of the abundance which I have made, and impart not his portion, according to the law of my gospel, unto the poor and the needy, he shall, with the wicked, lift up his eyes in hell, being in torment" (D&C 104:18).

As a body of Saints in the Church, we have a divine injunction to care for the poor and needy, the fatherless and widows.[83] Remember these words from our Savior Jesus Christ: "Verily I say unto you, Inasmuch as ye have done it unto one of the least of these my brethren, ye have done it unto me" (Matthew 25:40).

Regarding our preparation for the judgment day, President Dallin H. Oaks said, "This process requires far more than acquiring knowledge. . . . We must act and think so that we are converted by it. . . . The Final Judgment . . . is an acknowledgement of the final effect of our acts and thoughts—what we have become."[84]

In summarizing the purpose of the Final Judgment and how it should inform our actions in mortality, President Dallin H. Oaks taught,

> The purpose of this Final Judgment is to determine whether we have achieved what Alma described as a "mighty change of heart" (see Alma 5:14, 26), where we have become new creatures, with "no more disposition to do evil, but to do good continually" (Mosiah 5:2). The judge of this is our Savior, Jesus Christ (see John 5:22; 2 Nephi 9:41). After His judgment we will all confess "that his judgments are just" (Mosiah 16:1; see also Mosiah 27:31; Alma 12:15), because His omniscience (see 2 Nephi 9:15, 20) has given Him a perfect knowledge of all of our acts and desires, both those righteous or repented and those unrepented or unchanged.[85]

---

82   See Alma 4:13.
83   See James 1:27.
84   Dallin H. Oaks, "The Challenge to Become," *Ensign*, Oct. 2000, 40–41.
85   Dallin H. Oaks, "Cleansed by Repentance," *Ensign* or *Liahona*, May 2019.

CHAPTER EIGHT
RECEIVING PERSONAL REVELATION

Behold, I have fasted and prayed many days that I might know these things of myself. And now I do know of myself that they are true; for the Lord God hath made them manifest unto me by his Holy Spirit; and this is the spirit of revelation which is in me. (Alma 5:46)

THE PROPHET JOSEPH SMITH TAUGHT, "No man can receive the Holy Ghost without receiving revelations. The Holy Ghost is a revelator."[1] There is revelation in every aspect of the power and presence of the Holy Ghost. The Lord said, "Yea, behold, I will tell you in your mind and in your heart, by the Holy Ghost, which shall come upon you and which shall dwell in your heart. Now, behold, this is the spirit of revelation" (D&C 8:2–3).

After testifying with great power to the Nephites in Zarahemla, Alma asked his listeners, "Do ye not suppose that I know of these things myself? Behold, I testify unto you that I do know that these things whereof I have spoken are true. And how do ye suppose that I know of their surety?" (Alma 5:45).

It was, after all, a pivotal question: human nature causes us to be skeptical of one who so boldly

> ## ALMA'S QUESTIONS ON REVELATION
>
> Do you not suppose that I know of these things myself?
> (See Alma 5:45)
>
> And how do you suppose that I know of their surety?
> (See Alma 5:45)

professes to know things that are not accepted as common knowledge. Alma's audience did have knowledge of his remarkable conversion experience and may have been willing to credit part of what he was saying to the things that

---

1   *Teachings of the Prophet Joseph Smith*, sel. Joseph Fielding Smith [1976], 328.

transpired then. But Alma was not going to leave that to chance; he wanted not only to explain how he knew of what he spoke but to help his listeners learn that they themselves could receive the same kind of revelation he had known.

Setting out to answer how he knew with a surety the things of which he spoke, Alma said,

> Behold, I say unto you they are made known unto me by the Holy Spirit of God. Behold, I have fasted and prayed many days that I might know these things of myself. And now I do know of myself that they are true; for the Lord God hath made them manifest unto me by his Holy Spirit; and this is the spirit of revelation which is in me. (Alma 5:46)

Packed into that single statement is a veritable smorgasbord of staggering concepts. Alma began by telling his audience—then and now—that the things of which he spoke "are made known unto me by the Holy Spirit of God." Knowledge of Christ and the plan of redemption come only from the Holy Ghost, for "no man can say that Jesus is the Lord, but by the Holy Ghost" (1 Corinthians 12:3).

Those listening to Alma's explanation of the source of revelation may have reflected on his conversion experience—that startling episode when he was visited by an angel—and decided that such a heavenly visitation would certainly be more powerful than the seemingly fleeting impressions of the Holy Ghost. We might think the same thing.

Alma saw an angel, but he testified in Alma 5:46–47 that it was not seeing an angel, but fasting and prayer, through which he sought the Spirit of the Holy Ghost that allowed him to come to know the truth. President Heber J. Grant explained, "Many men say: 'If I could only see an angel, if I could only hear an angel proclaim something, that would cause me to be faithful all the days of my life!' It had no effect upon these men [Laman and Lemuel] that were not serving the Lord, and it would have no effect today."[2]

In underscoring the importance of the Holy Ghost in revelation, President Joseph Fielding Smith taught, "The spirit of God speaking to the spirit of man [through the Holy Ghost] has power to impart truth with greater effect and understanding than the truth can be imparted by personal contact even with heavenly beings."[3] He further wrote,

2   Heber J. Grant, *Conference Report*, Apr. 1924, 159.
3   "The Sin against the Holy Ghost," *Instructor*, Oct. 1935, 431.

The manifestations we might have of the Spirit of Christ, or from a visitation of an angel, a tangible resurrected being, would not leave the impression and would not convince us and place within us that something which we cannot get away from which we receive through a manifestation of the Holy Ghost. Personal visitations might become dim as time goes on, but this guidance of the Holy Ghost is renewed and continued day after day, year after year, if we live to be worthy of it.[4]

To remove any doubt that he was speaking by the power of the Holy Ghost, Alma then told his listeners that "the spirit of revelation . . . is in me" (Alma 5:46). Alma's statement can be taken literally; President Joseph Fielding Smith taught, "Through the Holy Ghost, the truth is woven into the very fibre and sinews of the body so that it cannot be forgotten."[5] Thus, true testimony is very literally internalized.

Alma, confirming that the spirit of revelation was in him, also indicates his profound degree of personal certainty about that of which he was speaking. His words were not the "idle mouthings of an iterant; nor were they the effervescence of zeal. . . . They were, however, his deliberate testimony—the sum and substance of his joy, happiness, and peace."[6] Alma later used this same phrase or a similar one—pointing to the testimony or the Spirit of God "which is in me"—throughout his speech to the Gideonites[7] and in his instruction to his son Shiblon.[8]

Other Book of Mormon prophets employed similar techniques to emphasize how deeply and personally they themselves *knew* the truths revealed in scripture. When confronting Sherem, Jacob said,

> Behold, I say unto you that none of the prophets have written, nor prophesied, save they have spoken concerning this Christ.
>
> And this is not all—it has been made manifest unto *me*, for *I* have heard and seen; and it also has been made manifest unto *me* by the power of the Holy Ghost; wherefore, *I* know if there should be no atonement made all mankind must be lost. (Jacob 7:11–12; emphasis added)

---

4 Joseph Fielding Smith, *Doctrines of Salvation*, comp. Bruce R. McConkie (Salt Lake City: Bookcraft, 1954), 1:44.

5 Joseph Fielding Smith, *Doctrines of Salvation*, comp. Bruce R. McConkie (Salt Lake City: Bookcraft, 1954), 1:48.

6 George Reynolds and Janne M. Sjodahl, *The Book of Alma, Chapters 1–26*, vol. 3 of *Commentary on the Book of Mormon*, arr. by David Sjodahl King (Salt Lake City: Deseret Book, 1973), 3:135.

7 See Alma 7:5, 16–17.

8 See Alma 38:6.

True testimony embeds itself deeply *in* the soul of a person; it is not a mere intellectual assent to a set of ideas. In his last general conference address before his death, Elder Bruce R. McConkie illustratively said,

> In speaking of these wondrous things, I shall use my own words, though you may think they are the words of scripture, words spoken by other Apostles and prophets. True it is they were first proclaimed by others, but *they are now mine*, for the Holy Spirit of God has borne witness to me that they are true, and it is now as though the Lord had revealed them to me in the first instance. I have thereby heard his voice and know his word.[9]

The Holy Ghost can also penetrate the very fibers and sinews of those who *hear* testimony borne through His Spirit. In a general conference address, Elder Joseph B. Wirthlin testified that "the Holy Ghost shall be shed forth in bearing record unto all things whatsoever [we] shall say."[10]

In addition to saying that the spirit of revelation was in him, Alma then testifies that the spirit of prophecy was also in him and that it too came through the Holy Ghost. "And moreover, I say unto you that it has thus been revealed unto me, that the words which have been spoken by our fathers are true, even so according to the spirit of prophecy which is in me, which is also by the manifestation of the Spirit of God" (Alma 5:47).

While the prophet is the only person who can receive revelation for the Church, those who are worthy of the Holy Ghost can receive and are entitled to receive revelation for their personal circumstances. In his general conference address shortly after becoming prophet, President Russell M. Nelson said,

> One of the things the Spirit has repeatedly impressed upon my mind since my new calling as President of the Church is how willing the Lord is to reveal His mind and will. The privilege of receiving revelation is one of the greatest gifts of God to His children. Through the manifestations of the Holy Ghost, the Lord will assist us in all our righteous pursuits.[11]

President Nelson went on to say,

> I urge you to stretch beyond your current spiritual ability to receive personal revelation, for the Lord has promised that "if

9   Bruce R. McConkie, "The Purifying Power of Gethsemane," *Ensign*, May 1985; emphasis added.
10   Joseph B. Wirthlin, "Pure Testimony," *Ensign*, Nov. 2000.
11   Russell M. Nelson, "Revelation for the Church, Revelation for Our Lives," *Ensign* or *Liahona*, May 2018.

thou shalt [seek], thou shalt receive revelation upon revelation, knowledge upon knowledge, that thou mayest know the mysteries and peaceable things—that which bringeth joy, that which bringeth life eternal" (D&C 42:61).[12]

Knowing that each worthy soul is entitled to personal revelation through the Holy Ghost, we can fully appreciate the words of Elder Bruce R. McConkie when he said,

> As starving men crave a crust of bread, as choking men thirst for water, so do the righteous yearn for the Holy Ghost. The Holy Ghost is a Revelator; he is a Sanctifier; he reveals truth, and he cleanses human souls. He is the Spirit of Truth, and his baptism is one of fire; he burns dross and evil out of repentant souls as though by fire. The gift of the Holy Ghost is the greatest of all the gifts of God, as pertaining to this life; and those who enjoy that gift here and now, will inherit eternal life hereafter, which is the greatest of all the gifts of God in eternity.[13]

President Wilford Woodruff taught that revelation is "the inspiration of the Holy Ghost to man."[14] The Prophet Joseph Smith said that the Holy Ghost "has the effect of pouring out pure intelligence upon [the worthy recipient]; all is calm and serene; the still small voice speaks peace to the spirit within man; and the sanctifying, cleansing power of the Spirit begins to manifest itself."[15]

Remembering the stunning visit of the angel to Alma and other dramatic accounts of revelation, we may mistakenly assume that revelation always comes in the same remarkable way. Such is not the case, and if we expect only that kind of experience, we can miss revelation that does come to us through the Holy Ghost. Elder Richard G. Scott taught,

> A communication to the *heart* [from the Holy Ghost] is a more general impression. The Lord often begins by giving impressions. Where there is a recognition of their importance and they are obeyed, one gains more capacity to receive more

---

12   Russell M. Nelson, "Revelation for the Church, Revelation for Our Lives," *Ensign* or *Liahona*, Apr. 2018.

13   Bruce R. McConkie, *The Mortal Messiah: From Bethlehem to Calvary* (Salt Lake City: Deseret Book, 1980), 3:122.

14   *Teachings of the Presidents of the Church: Wilford Woodruff* [2004], 50.

15   *Teachings of the Prophet Joseph Smith,* sel. Joseph Fielding Smith [1976], 149–150.

detailed instruction to the *mind*. An impression to the heart, if followed, is fortified by a more specific instruction to the mind.[16]

Revelation through the Holy Ghost can come in varied ways, many of which are subtle, depending on the purpose of the particular revelation. President Dallin H. Oaks identified eight different purposes or types of revelation: testifying, prophesying, comforting, uplifting, informing, restraining, confirming, and impelling. "Each of these refers to revelations that are received."[17]

President Wilford Woodruff taught concerning revelation,

> Joseph Smith said to Brother John Taylor in his day: "Brother Taylor, you watch the impression of the Spirit of God; you watch the whisperings of Spirit to you; you carry them out in your life, and [this] will become a principle of revelation in you, and you will know and understand this Spirit and power." This is the key, the foundation stone of all revelation. . . . In my own experience I have endeavored to get acquainted with that Spirit, and to learn its operations.[18]

The testimony of President Russell M. Nelson validates the role of the Holy Ghost as a revelator:

> As a member of the Quorum of the Twelve Apostles, I prayed daily for revelation and gave thanks to the Lord every time He spoke to my heart and mind. Imagine the miracle of it! Whatever our Church calling, we can pray to our Heavenly Father and receive guidance and direction, be warned about dangers and distractions, and be enabled to accomplish things we simply could not do on our own. If we will truly receive the Holy Ghost and learn to discern and understand His promptings, we will be guided in matters large and small. . . . I urge you to stretch beyond your current spiritual ability to receive personal revelation, for the Lord has promised that "if thou shalt [seek], thou shalt receive revelation upon revelation, knowledge upon knowledge, that thou mayest know the

---

16 Richard G. Scott, "Helping Others to Be Spiritually Led" [address given at the Church Educational System Symposium on the Doctrine and Covenants, Aug. 11, 1998].

17 Dallin H. Oaks, "Revelation," in *The Voice of My Servants: Apostolic Messages on Teaching, Learning, and Scripture*, eds. Scott C. Esplin and Richard Neitzel Holzapfel (Provo, Utah: Religious Studies Center, Brigham Young University; Salt Lake City: Deseret Book, 2010), 122.

18 *Teachings of the Presidents of the Church: Wilford Woodruff* [2004], 50.

mysteries and peaceable things—that which bringeth joy, that which bringeth life eternal." (D&C 42:61)[19]

OBTAINING SPIRITUAL KNOWLEDGE THROUGH THE HOLY GHOST

The Holy Ghost is the key to obtaining spiritual knowledge and the source of our spiritual rebirth, sanctification, and growth. He is the means by which we live an inspired life and the way through which we testify and know of God the Father and His Beloved Son Jesus Christ. It is the Holy Ghost that leads us "to do good—yea, to do justly, to walk humbly, to judge righteously" (D&C 11:12). The Holy Ghost will enlighten our minds and fill our souls with joy.[20] In our quest to obtain spiritual knowledge, we should follow the example of the Nephite disciples: "And they did pray for that which they most desired; and they desired that the Holy Ghost should be given unto them" (3 Nephi 19:9).

President Brigham Young emphasized the blessings of the fullness of the Holy Ghost when he said,

> If the Latter-day Saints will walk up to their privileges, and exercise faith in the name of Jesus Christ, and live in the enjoyment of the fullness of the Holy Ghost constantly day by day, there is nothing on the face of the earth that they could ask for, that would not be given to them. The Lord is waiting to be very gracious unto this people, and to pour out upon them riches, honor, glory, and power, even that they may possess all things according to the promises He has made through His apostles and prophets.[21]

The dedicatory prayer for the Kirtland Temple, given by revelation to the Prophet Joseph Smith, speaks of having this fullness of the Holy Ghost and the way in which it leads to spiritual knowledge. In the prayer, the Prophet Joseph prayed that all those who entered the Lord's house may not only seek knowledge out of the best books but that they "may seek learning even by study, and also by faith, as thou hast said; And that they may grow up in thee, and receive a fulness of the Holy Ghost . . . and be prepared to obtain every needful thing" (D&C 109:14–15).

That blessing is available to every one of us, then and now, because of the supernal gift of the Holy Ghost.

---

19   Russell M. Nelson, "Revelation for the Church, Revelation for Our Lives," *Ensign* or *Liahona*, May 2018.
20   See D&C 11:13.
21   Brigham Young, *Journal of Discourses* [1886], 11:114.

In his general conference address of October 1991, Elder Charles Didier spoke of how Alma gave "a perfect example" of the convincing spiritual knowledge he received by revelation as outlined in Alma 5:

> In four verses we learn about this light within [Alma]. First, the assurance of his testimony: "Behold, I testify unto you that I do know that these things whereof I have spoken are true." (Alma 5:45.) Second, the source of his testimony: "They are made known unto me by the Holy Spirit of God." (Alma 5:46.) Third, the process of gaining his testimony: "I have fasted and prayed." (Alma 5:46.) Fourth, the evidence of his testimony: "The Lord God hath made them manifest unto me by his Holy Spirit; and this is the spirit of revelation which is in me." (Alma 5:46.) Fifth, the origin of his testimony: "The words which have been spoken by our fathers are true." (Alma 5:47.) Sixth, the power of his testimony: "I say unto you, that I know of myself . . . that Jesus Christ shall come." (Alma 5:48.) This convincing knowledge or testimony would not be complete without also accepting the responsibility of carrying such a testimony. And Alma further stated, "I am called . . . to preach . . . to cry unto them that they must repent and be born again." (Alma 5:49)[22]

Remembering Elder McConkie's metaphor that the righteous yearn for the Holy Ghost like a starving man craves a crust of bread or a choking man thirsts for water,[23] we can and should develop that same kind of yearning for the Spirit. As we do, we will come to see how the Holy Ghost and His companionship will change our lives for the better.

As we obtain spiritual knowledge through the Holy Ghost, we will realize that it's impossible to live a Christ-centered life without the direction and power of the Holy Ghost in our lives. In his general conference talk of April 1965, Elder Delbert L. Stapley taught, "By inquiring of the Lord and listening to the voice of his Spirit and having a willingness to be guided thereby, we will always find ourselves on the Lord's side of every issue and be strengthened to defend and hold fast to that which is good and acceptable to our God."[24]

THE MISSION AND CHARACTERISTICS OF THE HOLY GHOST

Elder James E. Talmage taught,

---

22   Charles Didier, "Testimony," *Ensign*, Nov. 1991.

23   Bruce R. McConkie, *The Mortal Messiah* (Salt Lake City: Deseret Book Company, 1980), 2:122.

24   Conference Report, Apr. 1965.

The Holy Ghost undoubtedly possesses personal powers and affections; these attributes exist in Him in perfection. Thus, He teaches and guides, testifies of the Father and the Son, reproves for sin, speaks, commands, and commissions, makes intercession for sinners, is grieved, searches and investigates, entices, and knows all things. These are not figurative expressions, but plain statements of the attributes and characteristics of the Holy Ghost.[25]

In one of the earliest and most definitive Latter-day Saint statements about the mission and characteristics of the Holy Ghost, Elder Parley P. Pratt wrote that the Holy Ghost "quickens all the intellectual faculties, increases, enlarges, expands and purifies all the natural passions and affections; and adapts them, by the gift of wisdom, to their lawful use. It inspires, develops, cultivates and matures all the fine-toned sympathies, joys, tastes, kindred feelings and affections of our nature. It inspires virtue, kindness, goodness, tenderness, gentleness and charity."[26]

The words of both James E. Talmage and Parley P. Pratt testify that the power of the Holy Ghost benefits every aspect of our lives. When we are worthy and receptive, He becomes our Teacher,[27] our Comforter,[28] our Minister,[29] and our Sanctifier.[30] We teach and testify through His power, and we are taught through the same power.[31] Through this small sampling of the attributes and roles of the Holy Ghost, as well as those that follow, it is easy to understand why Paul referred to this great gift with such profound gratitude: "Thanks be unto God for his unspeakable gift" (2 Corinthians 9:15).

THE HOLY GHOST PURGES OUR SINS

We have been shown "the straitness of the path, and the narrowness of the gate" by which we can enter the kingdom of heaven (2 Nephi 31:9). That gate "by which ye should enter is repentance and baptism by water; *and then cometh a remission of your sins by fire and by the Holy Ghost*" (2 Nephi 31:17; emphasis added).

The "baptism of fire" by the Holy Ghost—not only at our confirmation, but each time we fully repent—purges our sins from our very being. We are literally

25   James E. Talmage, *The Articles of Faith* (Salt Lake City: Deseret Book, 1899), 144.
26   Parley P. Pratt, *Key to the Science of Theology* (Salt Lake City: Deseret Book, 1855), 98.
27   See Luke 12:12.
28   See John 14:26.
29   See Alma 19:14; Helaman 5:45; 6:36.
30   See 3 Nephi 27:20; Romans 15:16.
31   See D&C 68:3.

made clean and sanctified by the Holy Ghost[32] as our hearts, our minds, and our very souls are cleansed and made pure.

THE HOLY GHOST TEACHES US ALL THINGS AND BRINGS ALL THINGS TO OUR REMEMBRANCE

The Savior taught that "the Holy Ghost, whom the Father will send in my name, he shall teach you all things, and bring all things to your remembrance, whatsoever I have said unto you" (John 14:26).

Without the Holy Ghost, we cannot be taught nor can we learn eternal truths. The Holy Ghost teaches the things that will bring us closer to God and will help us follow our Savior Jesus Christ. He will teach us those things that will keep us on the covenant path. If we follow His teachings, we will always be in the right.

THE HOLY GHOST REVEALS THE MYSTERIES OF GOD

It had been more than a year since the Prophet Joseph Smith had started revising the Bible, a work that he went back to in January of 1832. Upon returning from a conference in Amherst, Ohio, in February of that year, he and Sidney Rigdon (acting as scribe) resumed the translation.

Joseph reported that during his study and translation work, as well as from the revelations he himself had received, it became obvious that many important truths about the salvation of man had either been lost or taken from the Bible before it was compiled. As he worked on translating the Gospel of John, he found himself puzzled by many questions and problems about the term *heaven*. The Prophet wrote, "It appeared self-evident from what truths were left, that if God rewarded every one according to the deeds done in the body the term 'Heaven,' as intended for the Saints' eternal home must include more kingdoms than one."[33]

After seeking answers to his questions on February 16, 1832, in the John Johnson home in Hiram, Ohio, the Prophet experienced a glorious vision regarding the three degrees of glory. That vision, which became section 76 of the Doctrine and Covenants, was given and received through the Holy Ghost. As Joseph related it, "By the power of the Spirit our eyes were opened and our understandings were enlightened, so as to see and understand the things of God" (D&C 76:12).

Sidney Rigdon saw the vision. Of the twelve or so other men in the room at the time, Philo Dibble related that he "saw the glory and felt the power, but did

32 See 3 Nephi 27:20.
33 *History of the Church*, 1:245.

not see the vision." As Dibble recounted the experience, he wrote, "Joseph sat firmly and calmly all the time in the midst of a magnificent glory, but Sidney sat limp and pale, apparently as limber as a rag, observing which, Joseph remarked, smilingly, 'Sidney is not used to it as I am.'"[34]

The mysteries of the kingdom (the doctrines), as evidenced in Joseph's experience with the vision recounted in section 76, are "only to be seen and understood by the power of the Holy Spirit, which God bestows on those who love him, and purify themselves before him" (D&C 76:116).

THE HOLY GHOST SHOWS US WHAT TO DO AND WHERE TO GO

Following a three-day conference at Fayette, New York, in September 1830, the Prophet Joseph Smith received a revelation for Thomas B. Marsh, who had recently been baptized and who was directed by the Lord to preach the gospel. In the revelation, the Lord said, "Go your way whithersoever I will, and it shall be given you by the Comforter what you shall do and whither you shall go" (D&C 31:11).

This same guidance and direction from the Holy Ghost occurs throughout the scriptures. Even the Savior was directed by the Spirit: "And Jesus being full of the Holy Ghost returned from Jordan, and was led by the Spirit into the wilderness" (Luke 4:1).

The Holy Ghost will show us all things to do[35] and will lead and guide us, even when we do not know ahead of time where we should go or what we should do.[36] Reflecting on that role of the Holy Ghost, President Wilford Woodruff taught the need of having the Spirit every day:

> Every day that we live we need the power of the Lord—the power of his Holy Spirit and the strength of the priesthood to be with us that we may know what to do. And if we will so live before the Lord, the Spirit will reveal to us every day what our duties are; I do not care what it is we are engaged in, we should first find out the will of the Lord and then do it, and then our work will be well done and acceptable before the Lord.[37]

THE HOLY GHOST LEADS US IN PATHS OF RIGHTEOUSNESS

In a revelation given through the Prophet Joseph Smith to his brother Hyrum at Harmony, Pennsylvania, the Lord said, "And now, verily, verily, I

---

34   Philo Dibble, *Juvenile Instructor*, May 1892, 304.
35   See 2 Nephi 32:5; D&C 39:6.
36   See 1 Nephi 4:6; Moroni 6:9; D&C 31:11; 45:57.
37   *Teachings: Wilford Woodruff* [2004], 52.

say unto thee, put your trust in that Spirit which leadeth to do good—yea, to do justly, to walk humbly, to judge righteously; and this is my Spirit" (D&C 11:12).

When we trust in the Holy Spirit, He will lead us to do many things in righteousness. The Holy Spirit works in concert with our faith, hope, and charity so that we are prompted to go about doing good.[38] We read that when the Nephites whom Jesus taught were baptized and received the Holy Ghost, they walked in paths of righteousness and dealt "justly, one with another" (3 Nephi 26:19). And we are told that as we are humble, the Lord will lead us by the hand.[39] The way in which the Lord leads us is through the power of the Holy Ghost.[40]

In his October 2015 general conference address, President Henry B. Eyring taught, "The companionship of the Holy Ghost makes what is good more attractive and temptation less compelling. That alone should be enough to make us determined to qualify for the Spirit to be with us always."[41] In that way, the Holy Spirit motivates us to change.

THE HOLY GHOST TESTIFIES

As we gain knowledge of God the Father and Jesus Christ, the Holy Ghost will testify of the truthfulness of that knowledge.[42] President Joseph F. Smith taught, "Without the aid of the Holy Ghost no man can know the will of God, or that Jesus is the Christ—the Redeemer of the world, or that the course he pursues, the work he performs, or his faith, are acceptable to God, and such as will secure to him the gift of eternal life, the greatest of all gifts."[43]

It is by the power of the Holy Ghost that we can be assured that we have found eternal truth, and it is by the same power that we can bear testimony of that truth. It is no light thing to be able to bear witness of God the Father and of the atoning sacrifice of His Son, Jesus Christ. The ability to so testify is evidence of our true conversion.

WE MUST LIVE SO THE SPIRIT OF REVELATION CAN WRITE ON OUR HEARTS

It is true that we have the *right* to receive the Holy Ghost when we are confirmed members of the Church following baptism—but if we want to enjoy

38   See Alma 7:24.
39   See D&C 112:10.
40   See 1 Nephi 4:6; 2 Nephi 32:5.
41   Henry B. Eyring, "The Holy Ghost as Your Companion," *Ensign* or *Liahona*, Nov. 2015.
42   See 2 Nephi 31:18; 3 Nephi 16:6.
43   Joseph F. Smith, *Gospel Doctrine: Selections from the Sermons and Writings of President Joseph F. Smith* [1986], 101.

His blessings, power, and constant companionship and experience the personal revelation available to us, we must be worthy. Throughout the scriptures, the following attributes are mentioned among those that help us be worthy of the companionship of the Holy Ghost:

Obedience. We need to be obedient and seek righteousness as we "*keep his commandments* which he has given [us]; that [we] may always have his Spirit to be with [us]" (D&C 20:77; emphasis added). Elder Marion D. Hanks said in his October 1967 general conference address that just as "we can desensitize a conscience, so to speak, so we can prepare ourselves better to hear the voice of the Lord by stripping off what the poet called the layers of 'muddy vesture and decay,' by ceasing to sin and learning to obey."[44]

Purity. We can purify ourselves through righteousness and the grace of God. The works of the Lord and the mysteries of the kingdom "are only to be seen and understood by the power of the Holy Spirit, which God bestows on those who love him, *and purify themselves before him*" (D&C 76:116; emphasis added).

Faith. We need to increase our faith in the Lord Jesus Christ. Lehi "spake by the power of the Holy Ghost, *which power he received by faith on the Son of God*" (1 Nephi 10:17; emphasis added).

Love of God. We need to love God with all our heart, might, mind, and strength. Remember that the things of God "are only to be seen and understood by the power of the Holy Spirit, *which God bestows on those who love him*" (D&C 76:116; emphasis added).

Remembrance of the Savior. We need to always remember our Savior Jesus Christ, as we are reminded to do when we partake of the sacrament: "And *always remember him* . . . that they may always have his Spirit to be with them. Amen" (D&C 20:77; emphasis added).

Meekness and Humility. Through the remission of sins that follows repentance, we become meek and lowly and are worthy of a visitation of the Holy Ghost.[45]

Prayer. We can plead in our prayers to be filled with the Holy Spirit[46] and to have the Spirit poured out upon us as well as the people we seek to teach and help.[47] Indeed, the Holy Ghost may respect human choice and agency so much that He patiently waits to be invited in. He is always a welcomed guest, but we must extend that welcome to Him before He can guide and bless us in a way that fully accomplishes the Father's will and purposes for us.

---

44   Conference Report, Oct. 1967.
45   See Moroni 8:26.
46   See Alma 18:16; Helaman 5:45.
47   See Mosiah 4:20; Alma 8:10; 19:14.

Endowment from on High. Alma Burton, former president of the Manti Temple, wrote, "Through the temple endowment, one may seek 'and receive a fulness of the Holy Ghost' (D&C 109:15)." In fact, "Temple ordinances are seen as a means for receiving inspiration and instruction through the Holy Spirit, and for preparing us to return to the presence of God."[48]

THE HOLY GHOST CAN FILL US WITH HOPE AND PERFECT LOVE

The Prophet Mormon wrote to us in our day:

> And the remission of sins bringeth meekness, and lowliness of heart; and because of meekness and lowliness of heart cometh the visitation of the Holy Ghost, which Comforter filleth with hope and perfect love, which love endureth by diligence unto prayer, until the end shall come, when all the saints shall dwell with God. (Moroni 8:26)[49]

Mormon's inspired words fill us with inspiration and hope. Repentance and the remission of our sins are not only the first steps to exaltation, but they help qualify us for the presence and power of the Holy Ghost. As we build a relationship with God the Father and depend on Him, we—like our Savior Jesus Christ—will be empowered by God and His grace and by the power of the Holy Ghost.

President Russell M. Nelson provided the ultimate hope when he counseled:

> When you reach up for the Lord's power in your life with the same intensity that a drowning person has when grasping and gasping for air, power from Jesus Christ will be yours. When the Savior knows you truly want to reach up to Him—when He can feel that the greatest desire of your heart is to draw His power into your life—you will be led by the Holy Ghost to know exactly what you should do.[50]

---

48   Daniel H. Ludlow, ed., *Encyclopedia of Mormonism* (New York: Macmillan, 1992), 455–456.
49   See also Romans 5:5.
50   Russell M. Nelson, "Drawing the Power of Jesus Christ into Our Lives," *Ensign* or *Liahona,* May 2017.

CHAPTER NINE
PREPARING EVERY DAY TO MEET GOD

Repent, all ye ends of the earth, for the kingdom of heaven is soon at hand; yea, . . . the King of heaven shall very soon shine forth among all the children of men. (Alma 5:50)

AMULEK, FAITHFUL MISSIONARY COMPANION TO Alma during much of his preaching to the Nephites, delivered a cautionary word intended to pierce our hearts and move us to swift action:

> For behold, this life is the time for men to prepare to meet God; yea, behold the day of this life is the day for men to perform their labors.
>
> And now, as I said unto you before, as ye have had so many witnesses, therefore, I beseech of you that ye do not procrastinate the day of your repentance until the end; for after this day of life, which is given us to prepare for eternity, behold, *if we do not improve our time while in this life, then cometh the night of darkness wherein there can be no labor performed.* (Alma 34:32–33; emphasis added)

Commenting on Amulek's counsel, Elder Quentin L. Cook said, "The scriptures are clear that while this life is relatively short, it is incredibly significant. . . . We do not want . . . to sleep through this life." He added that the scriptures "suggest that we should be true disciples of Jesus Christ. This entails establishing a powerful feeling of accountability to God."[1] Our time to prepare for eternity is, by definition, temporal, temporary, and limited. Procrastinating or putting off any righteous promptings to sincerely repent

---

1   Quentin L. Cook, "The Eternal Everyday," *Ensign* or *Liahona*, Nov. 2017.

is risky, if not dangerous, as Amulek warned. This is because we cannot know what opportunities for growth and progression will then pass us by or what inclinations or capabilities we will have to repent of on future occasions before we pass into eternity at the end of time. At that point, Alma tells us, we "shall rise again from the dead, which shall bring to pass the resurrection," to "stand before" God, in our bodies, "to be judged at the last and judgment day, according to [our] works" (Alma 33:22).

In his April 2018 general conference address, Elder Quentin L. Cook said,

> If, as individuals, we are really concerned about the Savior's ultimate judgment of us, we should seek repentance. I am afraid many people no longer feel accountable to God and do not turn to the scriptures or the prophets for guidance. . . . As Alma told his son Corianton in the Book of Mormon, "Wickedness never was happiness."[2]

That accountability to God does not happen only once every two years in our temple recommend interviews or during those times when we are issued callings or even once a year at tithing settlement; it is an accountability that should be exercised every day in our pleading communications with our Heavenly Father. As we establish that pattern of accountability, we recognize each new day as another day to prepare to meet God—another day to become more converted, to experience a greater change of heart, to more fully repent of any wrongdoing, to be constantly guided by the Holy Spirit.

It is that daily effort that will create of us disciples. The poet Edmund Vance Cooke, best known for his inspirational sonnets, penned a verse at the conclusion of the nineteenth century that has stark application to us in our day. The last stanza of "The Eternal Everyday" carries this timely caution:

> O, one might reach heroic heights
> By one strong burst of power.
> He might endure the whitest lights
> Of heaven for an hour;—
> But harder is the daily drag,
> To smile at trials which fret and fag,
> And not to murmur—nor to lag.
> The test of greatness is the way
> One meets the eternal Everyday.[3]

2   Quentin L. Cook, "Prepare to Meet God," *Ensign* or *Liahona*, May 2018.
3   Edmund Vance Cooke, *Impertinent Poems* (New York: Dodge Publishing Company, 1907), 21.

PREPARE QUICKLY, FOR THE KINGDOM OF HEAVEN IS "SOON AT HAND"

When can we expect the Savior's glorious return, the time when He will come "in his glory, in his might, majesty, power, and dominion" (Alma 5:50) to "put all enemies under his feet" (D&C 49:6)?

You know the answer. It is, simply, that we do not know.

Referring to His Second Coming, the Lord Himself said that "the hour and the day no man knoweth, neither the angels in heaven, nor shall they know until he comes" (D&C 49:7).

How, then, can Alma say that we "must prepare quickly; for the kingdom of heaven is soon at hand" (Alma 5:28)? He delivered these words approximately eighty-three years before the Savior was born—from our vantage, more than twenty-one hundred years ago. Such a span of time scarcely seems "soon at hand," even if it happened tomorrow.

But consider this: the very moment at which we pass from this mortal sphere is the very moment of *our* personal Second Coming—the very moment at which, for us, the kingdom of heaven is at hand. We do not know the hour and the day of that event any more than we know the hour and the day of the Savior's return to earth. Thus, Alma asks us, as he asked his audience in Zarahemla, a sobering question: could we say, if we were called to die at this time—*right now*—that we have sufficiently prepared, that our "garments have been cleansed and made white through the blood of Christ, who will come to redeem his people from their sins?" (Alma 5:27)

Can I say that? Can you say that? If not, Alma forewarns each of us, we "are not prepared to meet God," and we "must prepare quickly" (Alma 5:28).

Alma saying that the kingdom of heaven is soon at hand has several levels of meaning. One, of course, refers to the eventual establishment of the millennial kingdom over which Christ will rule and reign for a thousand years. Another refers to the Second Coming, the moment at which Christ will return to earth to usher in the Millennium. Or he may have referenced the Judgment Day at the end of time and the final resurrection. Even though we do not know the day and hour of those events, they may justifiably seem far distant, and we may be lulled into believing that we need not hasten our preparations.

The need to prepare quickly, however, was underscored by Elder Bruce R. McConkie, who reminded us,

> In another sense, the coming of the heavenly kingdom is equally close for men of all ages. This is so because those who live well

. . . irrespective of when they lived or how long they lived—will obtain citizenship in the heavenly kingdom hereafter.[4]

Wise is the man or woman who—while unable to predict the day and hour of a fatal heart attack or the course of a terminal illness or the sudden onset of a tragic accident or even the graceful decline of old age—prepares every day to meet God as if it were the last possible day or chance to prepare. To all of us, regardless of our circumstances, Alma says, "Repent, all ye ends of the earth, for the kingdom of heaven is soon at hand; yea, the Son of God cometh in his glory, in his might, majesty, power, and dominion . . . the King of heaven shall very soon shine forth among all the children of men" (Alma 5:50).

ALMA'S TESTIMONY OF THE SAVIOR

We can take Alma at his word because we can be assured that he *knows* the truths of which he testified. He did not start out on very solid ground, as we certainly all remember. But when a heavenly messenger intervened and warned him of the consequences of the path he was pursuing, this brought to remembrance that his father had spoken of "the coming of one Jesus Christ, a Son of God, to atone for . . . the world," and that led him to cry within his heart, "O Jesus, thou Son of God, have mercy on me, who am in the gall of bitterness, and am encircled about by the everlasting chains of death" (Alma 36:17–18). That crucial turning point ushered in Alma's spiritual transformation. He experienced a mighty change of heart and became a powerful prophet and witness. And he never looked back.

Knowing that, Alma's testimony of the Savior Jesus Christ in Alma 5 should penetrate our very souls: "I say unto you, that I know of myself that whatsoever I shall say unto you, concerning that which is to come, is true; and I say unto you, that I know that Jesus Christ shall come, yea, the Son, the Only Begotten of the Father, full of grace, and mercy, and truth. And behold, it is he that cometh to take away the sins of the world, yea, the sins of every man who steadfastly believeth on his name" (Alma 5:48).

Can we hear the infinite message Alma is sending us in our day? Jesus Christ, the Only Begotten of the Father, is coming. It does not matter when. It simply means that He is coming—and if we are prepared, if we work on our preparation every day, we will be numbered among those "who steadfastly believeth on his name."

---

4   Joseph Fielding McConkie and Robert L. Millet, *Doctrinal Commentary of the Book of Mormon*, Vol. 3 (Salt Lake City: Deseret Book, 1991), 43.

ALMA'S INVITATION TO US

Wrapping up his remarkable speech, Alma's final words in Alma 5 come in the form of both a commandment and an invitation—a command to those who belong to the Church and know the truth and an invitation to those still seeking that truth: "I speak by way of command unto you that belong to the church; and unto those who do not belong to the church I speak by way of invitation, saying: Come and be baptized unto repentance, that ye also may be partakers of the fruit of the tree of life" (Alma 5:62).

With his bidding, Alma reaches across the millennia to us—us for whom the Book of Mormon was written, preserved, brought forth, translated, and published. Referring to the rich doctrines of which he testified, he asks that we as members of the Church "observe to do the words which I have spoken unto you" (Alma 5:61). He invites every one of us to renew our covenants or to be baptized, uniting us in a bond of discipleship that will bring about a righteous community of Saints who are preparing together to meet God.

As we daily accept Alma's glorious invitation, President M. Russell Ballard reminds and assures us that we will qualify for divine assistance in our effort: "Every day of your life the Lord will help you if you trust in Him and keep His commandments. . . . Do what is necessary to build a real relationship with your Heavenly Father. You are His spiritual sons and daughters. Your divine parents love you with all Their hearts, as does the Lord Jesus Christ. They want you to follow the great plan of happiness that will lead you safely back home to Their presence."[5]

---

5   M. Russell Ballard, "Follow the Doctrine and Gospel of Christ," [Brigham Young University devotional, Nov. 7, 2010], 7, speeches.byu.edu.

ADDITIONAL REFERENCES

Baker, LeGrand L., and Stephen D. Ricks. "Alma 5: The Song of Redeeming Love." In *Who Shall Ascend into the Hill of the Lord?: The Psalms in Israel's Temple Worship in the Old Testament and in the Book of Mormon*, 2nd ed., 520–537. Salt Lake City: Eborn Books, 2011.

Barney, Kevin L. "Poetic Diction and Parallel Word Pairs in the Book of Mormon," *Journal of Book of Mormon Studies* 4/2 (Fall 1995):15–81.

Brown, S. Kent. "The Exodus Pattern in the Book of Mormon." *BYU Studies* 30 (Summer 1990):112–126.

Freedman, David N., ed. *The Anchor Bible Dictionary*. New York: Doubleday, 1992.

Kimball, Spencer W. "Circles of Exaltation," Address to Religious Educators, Brigham Young University, June 28, 1968.

Kugel, James L. *The Idea of Biblical Poetry: Parallelism and Its History*. New Haven and London: Yale University Press, 1981.

Maxwell, Neal A. "King Benjamin's Sermon: A Manual for Discipleship." In *King Benjamin's Speech: "That Ye May Learn Wisdom,"* eds. John W. Welch and Stephen D. Ricks, 1–21. Provo, Utah: FARMS, 1998.

McKay, David O. "Gospel Ideals," *The Improvement Era*, 1957.

Parry, Donald W. *The Book of Mormon Text Reformatted according to Parallelistic Patterns*. Provo, Utah: FARMS, 1992.

Perkins, Jerome M. "Alma the Younger: A Disciple's Quest to Become." In *Living the Book of Mormon: Abiding by Its Precepts*, eds. Gaye Strathearn and Charles Swift, 151–162. Provo, Utah/Salt Lake City: Religious Studies Center, Brigham Young University/Deseret Book, 2007.

Turner, Rodney. "Two Prophets: Abinadi and Alma." In *1 Nephi to Alma 29*, vol. 7 of *Studies in Scripture*, ed. Kent P. Jackson, 240–259. Salt Lake City: Deseret Book, 1987.

Welch, John W., Neal Rappleye, Stephen Smoot, David Larsen, and Taylor Halverson. *Knowing Why: 137 Evidences that the Book of Mormon Is True.* American Fork, Utah: Covenant Communications, 2017. This book, along with its 2019 sequel, contains several KnoWhy pertaining to Alma 5, along with others available at no charge on bookofmormoncentral.org and on the ScripturePlus app.

KnoWhy #113. "Why Did Alma Need to 'Establish the Order of the Church' in Zarahemla Again?" (in *Knowing Why*, pp. 260–262).

KnoWhy #112. "Why Did Alma Ask Church Members Fifty Probing Questions?" (pp. 258–229).

KnoWhy #111. "Why Did Alma Add 'Chains of Hell' to Abinadi's Phrase 'Bands of Death'?" (pp. 255–257).

KnoWhy #120. "Why Did Alma Talk about Melchizedek?" (pp. 277–279).

KnoWhy #136. "Why Did Alma Wish to Speak "with the Trump of God"? (pp. 314–315; Alma 29:1).

KnoWhy #144. "Why Was Alma Converted?" (pp. 32–35).

See also other relevant KnoWhys on bookofmormoncentral.org, such as:

KnoWhy #169. "Why Did [Captain] Moroni Refer to Vessel Impurity in Condemning the Central Government?"

KnoWhy #295. "Why Did Alma Ask about Having God's Image Engraven upon One's Countenance?"

KnoWhy #501. "What Does It Mean to Be 'Born Again'?"

ABOUT THE AUTHORS

ED J. PINEGAR IS THE author of more than sixty nonfiction books, audiobooks, and talks.

He has had the opportunity to teach at Brigham Young University, the Orem Institute of Religion, the Provo MTC, various seminaries, and BYU Education Week. He has been blessed with the opportunity to serve in many positions of leadership within The Church of Jesus Christ of Latter-day Saints, most recently serving as the Manti Temple president.

He and his wife, Pat, are the parents of eight, grandparents of thirty-eight, and great-grandparents of twenty-five. Ed and his wife live in Orem, Utah.

JOHN W. (JACK) WELCH LIVES with his wife, Jeannie, in Provo, Utah, where they have raised their four children and enjoy their seventeen grandchildren. He began teaching as a law professor at the BYU J. Reuben Clark Law School in 1980. During the last forty years, he has also served as the founding president of the Foundation for Ancient Research and Mormon Studies (1979 to 1989), as editor in chief of the academic journal *BYU Studies* (1991 to 2018), and one of the editors of the *BYU New Testament Commentary Series* (2008 to present), and as chairman of bookofmormoncentral.org (2016 to present).